DAILY TELEG
GUIDE TO RET

CW00428740

Daily Telegraph
Guide to Retirement

DAVID LOSHAK

Collins
London and Glasgow

William Collins Sons & Co Ltd
London & Glasgow

First published 1978
Latest Reprint 1978

© *Daily Telegraph* 1978
ISBN 0 00 412075 2 (limp)
ISBN 0 00 412077 9 (case)

Printed in Great Britain
Collins Publishers

CONTENTS

PREFACE

Retirement, says the *Oxford English Dictionary*, is 'withdrawal from occupation, office or business activity'. One purpose of this book, if the lexicographers will forgive such *lèse-majesté*, is to show that their definition of retirement is wrong.

I want to suggest a more constructive approach. Retirement, after all, is a phase of life which for many people these days lasts two decades or more – far longer than the years of formal education, or of adolescence, or even, in average homes, of bringing up a family. Yet the unhappy fact is that retirement is generally regarded as 'the end of the road' – a 'withdrawal', as the dictionary says. That word has an unfortunate connotation of a retreat into privacy or seclusion, as people spoke, in more formal days, of 'retiring' for the night.

To my mind, this is a dismal and depressing approach to retirement. No wonder a kind of taboo surrounds the whole subject of ageing, in the way we used not to talk about sex in polite society. But even if we think the pendulum has swung too far in being frank about sexual matters, no one argues for a return to earlier pruderies, and I feel that with age and its corollaries, the problems of retirement, people should stop pretending to themselves that they are exempt, that they can ignore such matters, that such things are better not considered.

For in fact the word 'retirement' suggests the total opposite of the truth. It is a time of life that can mean not a withdrawal but an expansion of activities and interests, a more fulfilling, not a more withdrawn, kind of life. Growing numbers of people are beginning to think that the autumn years of life can be the best, and should be regarded as Keats regarded the autumn season: one of 'mellow fruitfulness'.

Retirement, properly exploited, can give you greater freedom than you have ever had before to do what *you* want rather than do what your employer wants, or what your customers want, or what your family needs. You do not *have* to catch the 8.14 to town any longer.

But like any freedom, that freedom of choice can be a snare. The routine of everyday life provides a discipline which may seem irksome at the time but also keeps you – literally, in the case of commuters – on the rails. The extreme illustration of this is what happens to long-term inmates of hospitals or prisons when they are 'freed'. They have become 'institutionalized' and, unless prepared, are at a loss to run their own lives when released. To an extent, we are all institutionalized. When, on retirement, the chains of necessity and routine suddenly go, we are like children on the long summer holiday who ask: 'Mummy, do we have to do as we like?' Pools winners are another group who show similar symptoms: suddenly confronted by unlimited financial opportunity, they are often overwhelmed, and may either blithely squander the money, or waste it in another way by leaving it untouched.

It can be the same with retirement. An extension of freedom brings difficulties, drawbacks, problems and obligations of its own, and they too can be overwhelming. The period that is now coming to be regarded as 'the bonus years' provides not cash but a windfall of time. It can be misused as easily as any pools jackpot. Unless you are exceptionally lucky, you will not have enough money to do what you like or such a magnificent constitution that you can behave with the same disregard for your health as you did in your twenties. But you will have time. What I hope to show is that you do not need to be rich in retirement to avoid penury, that you do not have to be an athlete to enjoy relatively good health, that you do not have to be highly educated or exceptional in any other way to make the most of retirement. But you will have to know how to use the time it gives.

The secret is: preparation. It is learning how to make good use of the new-found lease of time, and not be over-powered by it. As with any other big venture, it makes sense to prepare for retirement just as we prepare, if we are prudent, for marriage or for a career. Indeed, if we regard retirement as a new career rather than, morbidly, as some form of 'withdrawal' from living, then we can see it and seize it for the opportunity it is.

Suggesting such a 'positive' approach will, I am sure, raise hackles on many who are looking forward to, or are even already enjoying, days of armchairs, pipes and cushions, people who no more thought of 'preparing' for retirement than they would think of 'preparing' to put on their trousers.

To those who find it both egregious and absurd that solemn 'experts' should teach them to suck eggs, who know they will be, or are, content to languish, who abhor mental or physical exercise let alone 'purposeful' occupation, whose only 'positive' want is to subside into a Nirvana of comfortable senescence, I say: 'Good luck'. Ignorance is bliss: they are a happy minority. Most of us are not made that way: if *you* were, you would almost certainly not be reading this book anyway.

The chapters that follow attempt, in a way that seeks to help without nagging, to see retirement in the same commonsense way that most people nowadays regard other matters (like atheism, say, or bodily functions) which earlier generations thought it more tasteful to camouflage.

The introduction will consider the context in which the whole matter of retirement is set. It will try to show in what way retirement is a problem, or at any rate a challenge, to our society. Unless we can understand that, we cannot properly decide the most effective approach towards it. The chapters that follow deal with the immediate and practical aspects of retirement: the problem of how to make the best use of time; the financial side; how to cope with growing older; the best use of leisure; where to live; how in general to get the most out of life. Finally, a reference section gives a range of organizations, sources of assistance, useful addresses and other background information.

It would, doubtless, be as well to admit at the start that this guide, written by a man, rather assumes that it is *men* who retire rather than women. This, of course, is not so. But it would be rather tedious if, at every point where the pronoun 'he' appears, 'or she' also had to appear. And, in everyday life, we do tend to think chiefly, in the family context, of the husband rather than his wife retiring, because that is the commonest situation that does arise. So it is not sexist or chauvinist, to use the current voguish epithets, to write primarily of the man's retirement. In any case, the effect of retirement on women has not been overlooked in this guide.

Likewise, this book is not solely for those who have

retired, or are near to retirement, but for younger people too, who rarely give a thought to retirement, which is natural. As with death and debility, we all sub-consciously think, when we are younger, that somehow retirement is not something that will affect us. But those in their 40s, 30s or even 20s who have the sense to realize that their 60s are not as far away as they seem, might find it useful to look through what follows.

In writing this guide, I have drawn on many sources for help. I have listened with great profit to Dr Alex Comfort, the gerontologist, Sir Ferguson Anderson, professor of geriatric medicine at Glasgow University, Dr James Hemming, the psychologist, Mr Fred Kemp, director of the Pre-Retirement Association, and others. I have learned much from the publications of the Pre-Retirement Association, Age Concern, the Royal College of Physicians, the Department of Health and Social Security, the Anchor Housing Association, the British Medical Association, the Elderly Invalids Fund, the British Geriatrics Society, the British Council for Ageing, Help the Aged, the National Council for Social Service, Barclays Bank, the British Association for Retired Persons, the Law Society, and others. I am grateful to the British Broadcasting Corporation and Alan Bennett for permission to quote from his play, 'Sunset Across the Bay'. I have also learned a lot from many publications, of which the most useful was *Choice*, the monthly magazine for those approaching, planning and enjoying retirement, and a self-renewing quarry of valuable information. My secretary, Miss Gulshan Chanara, has been of unfailing help.

David Loshak

INTRODUCTION

The age bulge

Every working day, some 1500 new pension books are sent out by the central pensions office at Newcastle on Tyne. Every year, 600,000 people retire. In Britain today, there are more than 8 million people of pensionable age – women over 60, men over 65. Every year, that number grows. The 'age bulge' will continue well into the next century.

The reason, simply, is the transformation of life expectancy brought about by modern health, nutrition and hygiene. In Christ's time, 30 was beyond the average expectation of life, as it is today in the more underdeveloped parts of Africa, Asia and South America. Two centuries ago, only six children in every 100 in Britain survived to the age of 60. One hundred years ago, life expectancy at birth was less than 50. Today, by contrast, a boy can expect on average to live to 69, and a girl to 75. Moreover, people who have reached those ages can expect on average to live another ten years. A quarter of them will live more than another 15. Not only are there many more people in their 60s, 70s and early 80s, but an even more rapid rise is taking place in the numbers who live until 90 and beyond. And it is *not* a fact that most of them are in geriatric wards or eking out medically synthetic half-lives.

None of this means, incidentally, that the human life span itself has lengthened. In Biblical times, it was 'three score years and ten, or by reason of strength four score years', and it is much the same today. What medicine and prosperity have done is to reduce the number of deaths in early life, enabling more of us to live to the end of the human life span. But that span has remained surprisingly unextendable so far.

The facts and figures make it dramatically clear, however, that the familiar concept of retirement at 60 or 65 is totally outmoded. At the time when the people now retiring were born, it was appropriate to think of them giving up work in their 60s, for the assumption was that they would, by that time, be worn out and 'old' with only a few quiet years left to live.

In fact, most of those who retire today can expect another 15, 20 or even more years of *active and healthy* life. This veritable social revolution has taken society by surprise. As a nation, we are singularly ill-prepared for it. The statistics show that people in retirement and approaching it are not at all unusual on that account. Yet society makes little allowance for them. The facts imply that no one who has retired should feel like an outcast from society, yet that is how older people are often made to feel.

A group of 8 million or more is a very large minority indeed, and hardly one, therefore, that should lack social, economic or even political consequence. If there were one concerted act that the retired and those approaching retirement could most usefully perform, it would be to jolt the nation towards a more realistic awareness of this issue. For society largely fails to recognize that retirement is no longer synonymous with old age, and that old age itself is largely a case of mind over matter: if you do not mind it does not matter. The penalties that are so widely associated with old age and retirement are far more the product of society's pre-conceived ideas than of biological ageing.

Increased average longevity means that the balance of the population is changing markedly. This will have profound effects. A different population make-up will impose different demands, social, cultural and economic, upon the community, and the human resources needed to meet those demands will change too. Society will need to come to terms with these changes to the same degree that individuals must come to terms with retirement if they are to make a success of it.

A promising way to do this would be to allow far greater scope than society readily offers at present to the retired to continue as useful members of the community. The 8 million would do well, therefore, to become better organized – even, indeed, more militant, so they can press effectively for due recognition of their social consequence and value. This is not to suggest the formation of yet another self-interested pressure group. It *is* to suggest that it is in the interests of our society as a whole that its older members should neither opt out of it nor allow themselves to be frozen out of it. They should instead help to enrich it by taking the most active possible part, and generate pressure in that way, so that their role may be more widely recognized as valuable.

Because nowadays there is a long, rather than a brief, interval between retirement and death, it is a fallacy to suppose that the moment people retire from gainful employment is the moment their old age begins. If true once, it is true no longer. Yet, society and governments have largely failed to plan rationally for this reality. This puts the ball in the individual's court, which may be the best place for it, as the individual is the most appropriate agent for determining his own lifestyle, even in an all-embracing welfare state (which Britain is not).

We have already touched on the practical reasons which should encourage people entering retirement to take the initiative in deciding the shape of their retirement years. The social change caused by the continuing growth in the numbers of older people over the next two decades could well prove a social disaster. The surest defence against that is self protection. The problem will be at its most acute among the over-85s, whose numbers, it is estimated, will increase by 40 per cent in the 20 years up to 1991, when they will total some 750,000. Through no fault of their own, such people will, because of their numbers, place ever greater strains on the medical and social services. There will be growing problems about how they are to be housed and cared for. The cost of this will have to be borne by that ever decreasing proportion of the population which is not dependent. We do not know, but can well guess at, the kind of political pressure that could build up against the major diversion of national resources that such demographic change will make necessary. It could all too easily result in the needs of the old not being adequately met by society in the future, if only because, ominously, they are not met particularly well even now.

Retirement fallacies

For such reasons, it makes both individual and social sense to plan for, and make good use of the retirement years. If the proportion of dependent or potentially dependent people is to grow to such an extent, then it is obvious folly to throw people on to a kind of social scrap heap when they reach a certain age simply because that age was regarded a century ago as old, while today it is nothing more than late middle age, and still very much the prime of life. To do that is to waste the skills and experience of those who are, quite possibly, among the most skilled and certainly, in the nature of things, are the most experienced. The value of elders to communities is keenly appreciated in most civilizations and cultures, yet underrated in our own. But even with us, judges, for example, are generally regarded as among the wisest members of the community, and are allowed to carry on working far beyond their 60s. Older people do not, however, have to be judges to possess such useful virtues as tolerance, punctuality, courtesy, patience, reliability, maturity and understanding. These virtues would merely be wasted if the retired who are fit – and they are the great majority – withdrew from work and other purposeful occupation.

Being older than 65 does not necessarily mean ill health, and does not even imply that inexorable physical and mental decline has set in. Of course, we all decline gradually from puberty onwards in different ways and at different rates. In some spheres, such as strenuous sports, even 30 is old. But the inevitable decrepitude once associated with anyone over the statutory retirement age is a myth today, and has been for far longer than is publicly acknowledged.

Most people begin to notice the ageing process around their 40s. Changes occur gradually: greying of the hair, development of longer sight, a certain loss of vigour and resilience (though a person's attitude can make a lot of difference on that score). But what really makes old age so difficult a time is not, as Alex Comfort has stressed, the failing of the flesh but the fact that society *imposes* a role on people simply because they happen to have reached a certain chronological age. They lose their jobs, they are placed in 'homes', they become the objects of pity and patronage as much as of respect. This is largely nonsense. The old, or the retired, are given their label regardless of individual merit or potential. Literally overnight, they are assigned a new role which diminishes their social status. While we have learned through experience how wrong it is to make sweeping generalizations about other minority groups, we still tend to do it with the over-65s. We still tend to think of them as 'past it'. Indeed, we still tend to think of ourselves as going to be 'past it' when we reach older age. Thus, it is a self-perpetuating fallacy, for once people have retired, they have often already brainwashed themselves into assuming that they will soon become infirm, soft in the head, slow to learn and incapable of sex.

Modern geriatric medicine teaches that such notions are utterly false. Ageing does not mean senility; being old does not mean that you cannot be contemporary; retirement does not mean the end or even the beginning of the end. Old people, says Comfort, are people who have lived a certain number of years, *and that is all*.

Nonetheless, the old attitudes persist. They are likely to stay because they are a deep-seated part of our way of life. So, retirement will remain a major watershed for everyone except those who never retire – chiefly, housewives and some of the self-employed.

Flexibility needed

Ideally, working life should flow imperceptibly into retirement over several years, with no clear division between the two. In practice, this would be tricky to arrange. There would have to be a major re-ordering of affairs in advanced, complicated economies such as ours. Some countries, nevertheless, have made a tentative start on schemes of flexible retirement, and the Council of Europe has taken up the idea, proposing that at retiring age, people should have a choice of continuing in a job. But to make sense, such a scheme must provide pensions that are high enough to ensure that people do not continue working solely to avoid a painful reduction in living standards. The Council of Europe acknowledges that there would have to be restrictions, which it does not yet specify, on the work and the type of work which people continued to do, because such matters as the employment situation and the need to protect health could not be overlooked.

The chances of bringing in flexible retirement on any scale look remote. A 1976 Government memorandum tartly dismissed the idea as 'not particularly promising' – a craven negativism apparently dictated by current financial constraints. The best that Britain could conceivably afford would be the option of a lower pension for those who retired early – but not its counterpart, a higher pension for those who retired late. In addition any 'partial pension' scheme, with people reducing their working week by stages, could cause problems with both unions and employers.

Even so, if other countries can solve such problems, Britain could. Our national pensions policy should surely be more flexible. Any 'retired person's lobby' of 8 million or more could do worse than make it a priority to force officialdom to be less stiff-necked about statutory pensions ages.

After all, in many spheres the move is towards earlier retirement. In some walks of life, like the armed forces and the diplomatic service, retirement in the 50s has long been accepted and retirement at 60 is routine in the civil service. There are clear reasons why the miners, for example, have been pressing to retire earlier, for their work is arduous in the extreme and can cost years of life.

But early retirement is not necessarily a boon. Retirement at 65 raises problems today that it did not in the past because many more people continue to live for an appreciable time. Extending that period by, say, five years hardly helps ameliorate those problems! Retiring early only makes sense if it is really early: probably not later than 55, so there is a real chance to develop a fully-fledged full-time second career. That apart, there should be a distinction, when talking of early retirement, between withdrawal from dangerous work, like mining, and retirement from work altogether. We would do better to think not so much of retiring earlier but of postponing retirement for those who are fit.

It is here that the Government could, and should, be more flexible. The way would be to make it customary to lighten gradually the physical and mental burdens. Were that more usual, no loss of face would be involved, if for example, a headmaster became an assistant master again at 57 or 62, or a director stepped back down into the sales force at 55 or 60. Miners would work at the face for no more, say, than 20 years, and thereafter continue only at the surface. In many other fields similar transitional arrangements could well be made, benefiting both individuals and the concerns for which they work. The skills and experience of those in their late 50s and 60s and even 70s should not be allowed to become redundant, especially in an economy such as Britain's, which is prone to crisis. If the fear is that deferred retirement for some would block the promotion of others below them, then career structures will simply have to be adapted. Surely such problems are not insuperable. Staff could be re-trained and sideways moves made easier. For example, a man who has worked as a skilled fitter might well, after years of experience in a factory, be invaluable in personnel or advisory work in the same company.

The pressure for early retirement is understandable in some cases. Thirty years on an assembly line, for instance, is probably more than enough for anyone, and it can be no hardship if they are terminated earlier. But in essence, the idea is short-sighted. The economic consequences of earlier retirement on a large scale would be crippling. Short-term financial gains, in pension terms, would sooner or later be outweighed by the long-term drain they imposed on the economy, with inevitable damage to the living standards of all, including the retired. Far better to defer retirement (for the fit) rather than retire early, not in our present work context but a context adapted, as suggested above, to the demographic facts of today.

Planning is vital

This is important on the individual level also. For those who are well-organized, early retirement could, when thoroughly well planned for, give even more 'bonus years'. Yet, most of us, without even realizing it perhaps, have most of our significance at work. Most of our friends are there. We act out our roles there. Many of the little dramas of life are played out there. To break the habits of a lifetime to fulfil retirement fantasies – living in the 'dream cottage', enjoying long-postponed experiences, spending the carefully accumulated (but easily depleted) nest egg – is really asking for trouble.

Often, indeed, such 'fantasy' retirement, especially a retirement for which nothing is intended but unending, and therefore stultifying, 'leisure', leads with surprising speed to premature death. This is not sensationalist, but a simple matter of medical fact. Doctors know that sudden death does sometimes come to perfectly fit people soon after retirement. They cannot wholly explain it, but it clearly has something to do with the sudden removal of the work pattern and the failure to adjust. And that, of course, springs almost certainly from inadequate preparation for retirement. The will to live goes because much of the reason for living has gone. Some doctors even write 'sudden death retirement syndrome' on death certificates because no more conventional medical reason can be found. They could more truthfully give the cause of death in such cases as 'broken heart' or merely 'boredom'.

It is extraordinary that we prescribe and actually legislate for compulsory retirement ages when all we really know about the effects is that we are largely in the dark about them or that they are harmful, even fatal. Those most at risk are the men who strive, through dedication to their work, to make themselves indispensable. But once retired, such people suddenly realize they are not as badly needed as they thought. They once filled their lives with their work, bringing it home in briefcases for the evenings and at week-ends. They had no other interests. Now, after retirement, they are the leading candidates for an early grave.

By contrast, the 'low risk' man has prudently assessed his budget and the effect retirement will have on it. He has worked out the value of his State and other pensions, any income from post-retirement work, either full or part-time, and the effects of that income on his tax and pensions. If he has prepared well, he will already be participating in activity outside work, both recreational and vocational – in local government, perhaps, or on the community health council or in any of the multifarious voluntary organizations and agencies. The range of possibilities is limitless, and these activities can be stepped up after retirement. His home, diet and the very tempo of his life will *not* drastically change. Retirement will mean that he no longer lives for his work, nor has to work in order to live. It can mean the best of both worlds.

This brings us back, yet again, to the inescapable fact that only a prepared retirement can be successful. Retirement does mean a major change, for men who have had a job or a career for 40 years or more will suddenly be out of the mainstream. People know one another by their occupations: I am a writer, you are an estate agent, manager, company director, salesman or whatever; he, or she, is something else again. At retirement, we are merely ex-managers, ex-salesmen and so on. For a woman, the change can be as abrupt as for a man. Even if she has spent her life as a housewife, and continues to do so, she will now have her husband around very much more of the time, and unless he is purposefully occupied in ways suggested later in this book, then his retirement can be very difficult for her to handle too. Retirement creates, in short, what the psychologists term an 'identity crisis' no less traumatic than adolescence. The retired can suffer a loss of status, a loss of value. They are suddenly outsiders. In Alan Bennett's play, 'Sunset Across the Bay', a couple move on their retirement from Leeds to Morecambe, a fatal mistake, as we will consider in Chapter 2. They go to an old folks' meeting where a hearty lady gets them to sing a fatuous song called 'I am H-A-P-P-Y', and when they come home, the husband, a down-to-earth working class man who is no intellectual but certainly no fool, says sadly to his wife: 'Three months since, I was doing a responsible job. Now I'm fit for nowt but clapping hands with a roomful of daft old lassies'. A little later, his wife says of him that he won't settle down and get used to being retired at Morecambe. As Alan Bennett deftly shows in two or three poignant little scenes like these, retirement for people who are not prepared can be a bitter and a shattering experience. Before long, the mentally shrivelled fellow simply curls up and quite needlessly dies.

Opportunity and fulfilment

But a good education or cultural background is not a pre-requisite for exploiting and enjoying retirement to the full. Obviously, the person who already has a wide range of interests, a catholic appreciation of the arts, a lively mind, has excellent basic equipment with which to embark on retirement. But also for the man or woman who left school at 14 or 15 and has never again found a chance to repair the damage of an unfinished or a botched education, or to explore new avenues, retirement is a wonderful opportunity. Aeschylus said that 'it is always in season for old men to learn', and the only thing wrong with that was that he left women out. The normally healthy brain does not, contrary to widespread popular belief, deteriorate with age. The capacity for learning remains. Of course, a mind that has not been used will, like any muscle, go flabby with neglect. But it can be revitalized. Some holier-than-thou pushers of 'purposive' retirement cite such examples as Bertrand Russell conducting high-level public debate in his 90s, Shaw writing plays at 93, Schweitzer building roads at 88, Rubenstein playing more brilliantly than ever at 89, Golda Meir leading Israel at 75, Grandma Moses taking up painting at 78 and becoming internationally acclaimed, and so on. But such people were outstanding in their younger years too. We cannot hope and do not seek to emulate the achievement of the outstanding, and citing them as examples is not all that inspiring because their experience is not relevant to ordinary people. The real point is that achievement according to our own lights need not be exceptional in later years, and there are indeed innumerable cases of everyday people who are publicly unknown who have learned new languages, acquired new skills, broadened their horizons in all kinds of exciting ways while in their 60s, 70s or even 80s. Some people, of course, may be handicapped, physically, financially, intellectually, or because of some other personal circumstance. But such handicaps are surmountable more often than not, and the biggest handicap of all to a successful retirement is none of these things: it is a self-imposed sense of apathy or defeatism. Those who approach retirement need only to come to terms with the fact, and to see it as a time for discovery and re-discovery, for filling in the gaps left earlier in life and for finding new gaps to fill in later life.

A word, however, of caution. It can be more futile

than fruitful to chalk up in advance all kinds of experiences which you intend to savour in retirement. When the time comes, you may feel an unnecessary sense of obligation to pursue the deferred interest or activity even if it no longer has the same attraction or has lost its relevance. Retirement is not for doing what 'ought' to be done, and it can be a mistake to stick doggedly to pre-determined courses instead of living for now. Experiences cannot be stored up for later use. The more you have, the more you have left.

The familiar ritual of presenting those who are retiring with a watch or clock could hardly be more inappropriate, because for the first time in life, time ceases to be the governing factor. Yet, totally wrong attitudes persist, symbolized again in the design of so many retirement cards, crassly depicting a setting sun. The terms associated with retirement are wrongheaded: 'retirement' itself, as we have seen, is a misnomer. 'Old age pensioner' is perhaps the worst, implying both senility and dependence, but 'senior citizen', if an improvement, has acquired the stigma of all such euphemisms and underlines the supposed lack of status of the old by mocking it.

The term which should most be associated with retirement has been appropriated by the young: 'coming of age'. In fact, most people become fully adult for the first time only when they retire, for it is then that they alone, not parents, teachers or employers, are masters of their destiny.

And this, of course, is why problems arise, as well as opportunities. Retirement does mean dismissal and unemployment. The way to prepare for it, then, is as you might prepare for dismissal and unemployment.

A sense of purpose and achievement is essential to well-being, and in adult life the chief source of these, along with home and recreation, is work. Therefore, a work vacuum, consisting only of the kind of 'leisure' that is pre-packaged, is all right for a week or two, but is too trivial and unsatisfying, even for the most undemanding people, as a long-term proposition. A life without purposeful activity will often lead to pre-occupation with self, morbid introspection, a heightened awareness of minor discomfort, a crotchety old age.

Through forethought, that course is eminently avoidable. We can ensure that retirement is a time of opportunity, not restriction; of fulfilment, not decline; of enjoyment, not depression; of participation, not vegetation; of self-determination, not dependence.

A guide to how this might be ensured now follows. We start where retirement starts, at home, and consider how the new life will affect family relationships. This leads on to a look at the question of where that home should be, and then to discussing some of the possibilities for using the time at home that will now be available. This clearly depends in part on financial considerations, the matter which probably bulks largest in the anxieties of the retired and those approaching retirement. Those anxieties, of course, can continue to be a worry right through retirement, especially in times of inflation.

One way in which the financial problems of retirement can be ameliorated is by work, and Chapter 5 considers the occupations, paid and voluntary, open to the retired. But how active a retirement can be does depend on health, so Chapter 6 examines this in all its aspects as it affects the retired. Before the final reference section, we consider the mechanics of preparing for retirement.

I

YOUR FAMILY – AND YOURSELF

Retirement and marriage

When a man retires, it is his wife and family who can suffer the worst 'withdrawal' symptoms.

For 40 or more years, in all probability, the husband and father has never been a full-time husband or father. A large slice of his waking hours, even with week-ends and holidays taken into account, has been spent at work. Retirement means that a man comes to *live* full-time at home for the first time.

Even in the happiest, most companionable of families, this can place great strains on relationships. A woman's life becomes entirely different when her husband is around all day, every day. Yet, while for her it is a disruption of a life-long routine, whether she has been a housewife or a career woman, for him it can mean finding that, somehow, he is a stranger in his own home.

For them both, unless he finds full-time work after retirement, life is radically changed. Marriage itself shows that propinquity can be a most testing situation. Retirement intensifies that. The only good approach is an understanding and aware preparation. It needs a readiness by all involved to see what difficulties could arise, followed by a readiness to adjust one's ways in order to cope with them, and a willingness to discuss matters frankly.

Clearly, this is not something that can be done suddenly or even in the two or three years before retirement. The way a person is in retirement, the kind of relationships he has, the way his retirement affects his nearest and dearest, depend totally on the sort of person he was before retirement, and the kind of relationships he developed over a lifetime. Loners will tend to remain loners. Those whose companionships were largely at work may suddenly feel bereft. But the man who developed interests and contacts outside his work will still have them when he himself is outside of work.

A marriage that has, perhaps, hung together for years 'for the children's sake' or on some other tenuous basis is clearly at the greatest risk after retirement, and divorces of couples in the 70s and 80s are no longer a great rarity. For years, a man may have found release and 'escape' at the office, while his wife may often have been relatively 'free' during the day. But while it is possible to work for years alongside colleagues you may not particularly like, endless domesticity with someone who is incompatible is infinitely more difficult.

Yet even though such couples may not have been ideally happy, nor have they separated, despite everything. Now, comparatively late in life, their need for each other is probably greater than either realizes. Incompatible they may be, but familiar to one another also: they are a unit, and their identity is inescapably bound up in that unit – family, friends, home, possessions.

So, it must be faced: retirement can put a marriage under great strain. Yet, it can also mean a fresh start, a second honeymoon. It is an opportunity to avoid the worst of things or make the best of things. This requires foresight, forethought and frankness.

One key to good relationships is, of course, consideration. The husband who is planning his retirement must think of the effect of his plans on his wife.

He may want, for example, to study brasses in parish churches round the country, or photograph owls. Fine, provided church brasses are not a passion in which his wife is utterly uninterested, or provided she realizes and accepts that he may often be out until dawn! He may have plans to spend all his time at home, working on some pet project, but to what extent will that tie his wife down to preparing daily lunch as well as dinner? That is a lot of extra work, and ought not just to be taken for granted. How might it, also, affect the routines *she* has built up, of which his absence at work has left him largely unmindful? Many such things which can be taken as read are brought right to the surface by retirement and have a surprisingly sharp impact on day-to-day living.

There are, of course, the ideally retired couples who seem to have it all worked out. They do the shopping and the gardening together, they share the same interests and enjoyments, and the chores like washing up and house cleaning. But again, it must be faced: sooner or later, bereavement must come. Then, will a widow be able to cope with the legal and financial problems that may ensue, with aspects of their affairs that have, for all their sharing, been overlooked? Will a widower be able to clean and iron his shirts, cook his meals, sew on buttons? There is no need to be morbid in acknowledging as a reality that in a partnership, one partner will one day die, and then to recognize that, while interdependence is admirable, it fails in a crucial way if it ultimately boils down to mere dependence because of a failure to see to it that each partner can be independent, when the need arises. This again is something that ought not be taken for granted.

Take another case. The helpful husband, now around the house all day, can, in a way, be over-helpful, a bit of a nuisance. And the over-dutiful wife can be, in practice, something rather like a nag. For it is fatally easy for people to get on one another's nerves in retirement. Convention leads us to believe that this is not so, but it is. Strains arise because a couple are suddenly together, quite possibly under circumstances that are not, for all their dreams and hopes, ideal, and for very much more time than they have ever been used to. So, a husband who 'helps' by re-organizing the kitchen on more rational lines may succeed only in upsetting his wife if, as is likely, she likes the existing arrangements, even if they do seem a muddle to anyone else. The husband who 'helps' only when the mood takes him but not otherwise, who will occasionally 'help' by cooking an exotic supper that leaves the kitchen a shambles, but rarely if ever really helps by offering to scrub the potatoes, is not, of course, doing anything to help at all. Actually, he is being selfish, helping himself to some satisfaction and probably helping to set his wife's nerves in a frazzle.

But a wife can 'kill with kindness' too. The woman who has spent half a lifetime bringing up a family may, now that the children are grown up, 'mother' her retired husband instead. There are many more such situations, fraught with potential problems for the retired in their relationships. The sensible course is to see the other partner's point of view, not solely by thinking to oneself about it, but by talking things through, in advance, on a basis of candour, affection and respect.

That is easy to say but difficult for most people to do. We are largely poor at discussing our relationships with one another. Indeed, many are unsure of themselves, let alone their relations with others, and perhaps at no time more than retirement, a period which can be as full of uncertainties and self-revelation as adolescence. All the more reason, then, for mutual consideration of the matter. If, as is quite likely, discussion is difficult, then one aim of this book is to help break the ice.

When a man retires, a couple spend something like eight hours a day more together than before. The retirement that for a man means more freedom can for his wife mean immense loss of freedom.

Yet many men are unaware of that possibility. In the past, the wife could plan her day to fit in with her husband's absence. Now, he must *always* be taken into account. The more active she was, both in the home and in such outside interests as meeting her friends, visiting the library, playing cards, doing voluntary work, the more her newly home-tied husband can intrude into her settled routine.

The answer is not that she must do all the adjusting, nor must he: it is, again, something they need to adapt to together.

This is particularly important for the growing numbers of retiring people who have many interests to pursue and who plan an active, vigorous retirement rather than a sedentary one. As much as at any other vital time in life, it is essential that husbands and wives consult one another. Is the wife of the keen gardener content, that for much of his time he will be out at the back, leaving her on her own? If not, they must think what to do about it, for clearly it would not be fair for him to give up the whole idea. It is this kind of situation, which can take innumerable other forms, that they need to work out together beforehand. That can ensure that retirement does not, cause contention, recrimination and resentment, as it so often does. For, in the example just given, the wife would understandably resent the apparent fact that her husband was more interested in the garden than in her. Such feelings can only corrode their relationship. Should he then seek to retrieve the situation, by not devoting himself to the garden so much, he could well feel resentful in his turn, and thus unnecessary misunderstanding feeds on itself.

Shared experience

The most vital and lasting companionship, in fact, comes from *sharing* activity. This can be something in which both partners have an interest before retirement, or something totally new that attracts them both. There are myriads of possibilities, of course, besides that cliché of retirement, gardening, satisfying and pleasant as that can be. Indeed, there are as many possibilities as there are aspects to life itself. Retirement need not narrow your horizons. The retirement years can open up wider possibilities for fulfilling activity for both husband and wife than any other period in life – provided the domestic basics are got right.

The single

There are some, of course, who cannot share. But even for widows, widowers and the unmarried, there is much to look forward to in retirement. A lot depends on whether or not the single person has, earlier in life, cultivated or neglected to cultivate interests and friendships. A word here, incidentally, on what we mean by friendship. As Alex Comfort has said, if friendship means a satisfying or lasting relationship, then it must involve a higher peak of shared experience than playing golf or a pint at the pub. And in a work-orientated society like ours, it is folly not to cultivate post-retirement friendships before retirement. For the single retired person who has always been a loner, who is inward-looking and perhaps inclined to self-pity, retirement will only intensify loneliness, while those who have been outward-going in earlier years, who have accumulated friends and even god-children in good number – they will have little difficulty in living lives replete with happy relationships. Finally, the single person has one great advantage at retirement: he does not have any-thing like the same problems of adjusting as his married colleagues.

For the widow or widower, adjustment can be doubly difficult. This is because it must be on the emotional as well as the practical plane. The dissolving of the marriage 'unit', already referred to, comes at the same time as the other main anchor of life is pulled up. A move to another home may now become unavoidable, particularly if the prospect of living alone is too daunting for the surviving partner, as it very understandably can be for those who have never lived on their own before. Coping with bereavement is something that must ultimately happen in all lifelong relationships, and is therefore a matter with which we must deal in a later chapter.

Grandchildren

On a more cheerful level, there is the role played in the life of the retired by their grandchildren, so often a source of great happiness. But not, alas, inevitably: it can at times be difficult for grandparents to understand, let alone approve of, the way their grandchildren are raised. Ideally, parents understand anxieties of this kind that the grandparents may feel, and allow for them by not being inflexible. But the grandparents, too, must make allowances. It may be easy for them to forget the practical difficulties involved in bringing up young children - problems over meals, bathtime, bedtime, television, mischief, nightmares and all the rest of it - and so look back on their own experiences, decades previously, in a rosy, nostalgic glow. It is often good that they can! But this can obviously mislead, so they should not seek to have a direct responsibility for the rearing of their grandchildren.

In any case, it is not a function they can adequately perform, however tempted they may feel to do so (except in those cases where, through some family misfortune, they become parents by proxy). Instead, they can sit back a bit. They do not *need* to interfere. This does not mean that the only role assigned to them is that of being boring old folk always talking about the past - though a living link with the past is something that children almost instinctively find fascinating. But grandparents can also become closely involved with their children's children in a mutual exploration of the world around them, having a common interest in so many things from an afternoon's outing in the park or to a museum, to going together on holiday or discovering literature. From such as this, all the generations can win enrichment, and have a relationship which is satisfying to them all. But it is for the parents, not the grandparents, to actually bring up the children, teaching them how to behave, deciding when they must have a bath, and so on. It is the grandparents, more relaxed, with more time and more experience, freed from the daily routines of parenthood, who can often best communicate with the young. And children, of course, usually love their company. So, it is a relationship to be savoured and fostered. Grandparenthood is, surely, one of the very greatest joys of retirement.

Successful relationships are a two-way process. But at least half of the responsibility for their success, perhaps more, lies with the retired person, who can be presumed, one trusts, to have the greater measure of maturity and tolerance. Yet, we already know of the acute sense of loss of status that retirement can bring, and so there can be an irresistible temptation for many who retire to compensate for that loss by being hyper-critical, intrusive, interfering. 'In my day, we did it this way,' and so on. Nothing irritates younger generations more than an approach of that kind. However good such advice may be, it will be unacceptable if proferred in a carping or hectoring form by someone whose manner makes him appear 'an old bore'. The young are *not* antagonistic towards the old, but can be as antagonized by them as by bores of any age. The approach must be one which inspires trust, not irritation; there must be a willingness to give support and help, but it must be in a contemporary context, not one of harping on 'the good old days' (which we surely know in our heart of hearts were never as good as they are painted).

Balanced attitudes

Just as vital is a balanced approach to the new life-style which retirement has brought about. It is not merely pointless to resent being retired – it is positively self-defeating. The retired person who nurses a grudge about his retired condition is as unconstructive as those who are forever harking back to the past. Approach and attitude govern mental health, and mental health is a vital factor in physical well-being. Unhappy people ache more – at any rate, they notice their aches more (which is much the same thing). It is better to be in charge of one's destiny to the fullest possible extent: a negative, self-defeated person cannot do it to any extent. The positive approach, in other words, pays off, and not only in that way, for there are other aspects – less self-indulgence in diet and in habits like smoking and lack of exercise is self-discipline of another kind which can mean that death, which ultimately must come, does so at the end of life, not merely at the end of 'old age'.

The attitudes of wives are vital, too. As the children grow up and leave home, women owe it to themselves to develop pursuits outside the home. Otherwise, they are in danger of becoming housebound cabbages. Although, obviously, they should not 'nag', nor should they over-indulge their husbands. Over-feeding, for example, however enjoyable, is really nothing better than a form of malnutrition, and is just as fatal as chronic under-nourishment.

Many retired people live alone, and for them, retirement can be more difficult than for any others. Complaints about loneliness are very understandable. But many who do not *live* alone are, nevertheless, lonely, too, for they have isolated themselves. Theirs is a subjective rather than an objective loneliness. They are not interested, or do not show interest, in the world around them, in new things, new ideas, new developments. They even display a reluctance to know what is going on in their own families. 'I don't understand these funny new gadgets – in my day we didn't need this kind of thing.' Such an approach is disastrous. Today is as much 'my day' for the retired person as any past day. It is there to be lived. There is no necessity to understand everything new, let alone approve of it. But to be uninterested and walled-off, to affect a tetchy, pernickety disdain of all that is contemporary solely because it is so, merely sets a retired person apart from the rest of his fellows, and makes him a permanently grumpy and disgruntled 'old buzzard'.

Such an attitude squanders rewarding opportunities for closer relationships. This is not to suggest that the older person should not offer advice or even criticism – 'pulling rank' (to take a military metaphor) is one of the privileges of retirement. But there are ways of doing it. If it is done solely to justify one's own fossilized conservatism or inability or unwillingness to learn and to adapt, the motivation is wrong. Such lack of genuine concern will show. Again, the words in which advice is proferred can make all the difference. Suggestions which begin with 'Surely . . .' or 'In my day . . .' are certain to backfire.

Understanding others

Finally, the retired might, I suggest, seek to enter the minds of those younger than themselves. They might try to understand how the young regard them, and make allowances accordingly. Perhaps that is a counsel of perfection, but it remains true that it can be very difficult for relatives like, for example, the daughter of a retired person, already more than adequately burdened with a family and perhaps a career of her own, to be fully aware of her parents' problems in their retirement, let alone to be understanding and sympathetic.

Nothing, perhaps, is worse than absence of concern, but care which is exceptionally devoted can be hard to take as well. From the perspective of those who give it, it is difficult to appreciate how much a regime of doting care can undermine a retired person's independence, and how important that independence is. The erroneous assumption that a retired person must be infirm to some degree is today largely denied by the facts, but it is a belief that is still widely held. So, people strive 'to look after' their retired elders, and to retired people who are basically fit this can seem irksome and patronizing, even humiliating. As with other tricky personal aspects of retirement (and in life generally, for that matter), such problems are best resolved by talking them out in an atmosphere of frankness and affection, and retired people can help by knowing and understanding in advance that such are the situations that can develop as the years go on.

So it is not necessarily the best course for retired people to go to live with sons and daughters. Because retirement is a new start in life, many feel that, on retirement, the best course is to move to a new place altogether. That can be a very happy experience but, again, not necessarily. Let us now consider the pros and cons of moving home on retirement.

2

A HOME FOR LIFE

Where to live

Your retirement home is, more likely than not, the
home you will have for the rest of your life. The kind of
home you have is fundamental to your well-being at
any age, but in the years of retirement, it is more
important than at any other time. This is so because
home is the focus of your life more than ever before. The
choice of where to live is therefore crucial for the success
of retirement.

The difficulty is that the choices are many. The
variables that must be considered are bewildering in
number and complexity. Finance and health are
obviously important factors that must influence, and may
govern, the choice you make: further details on both
those counts are discussed in later chapters. If you
continue to work, this will probably limit your choice of
where to live. But if you do not, there may be a large
array of alternatives to think about. Do you stay put or
move? If the former, will your present house be manage-
able? Or should it be converted in some way? If you
move, do you go to other accommodation in the same
district or move to a different district? If the same
district, do you take a house, a bungalow or a flat?
Or do you share with relatives? If another district, in
Britain or abroad? If in Britain, in town, or in the

country, or by the sea? If abroad, which country, and what are the legal, financial and social considerations? The question of whether to opt for sheltered accommodation, that is, housing with some form of special care provided, might also need thinking about. And this by no means completes the range of questions that might need to be asked and answered.

For some, these problems of retirement may well have solved themselves by the time retirement actually comes. Illness or money problems may dictate the 'choice' to be made. Or, a more far-sighted couple may already have moved well before retirement, into more compact accommodation. This might well suit them for years after retirement as well as before it.

But for most, retirement is the first time since the early years of a career or of marriage when major questions about where and how to live arise. Many feel that this fresh start in life merits a complete change of locale. Getting away from the familiar can indeed prove a stimulating and happy decision, but it is one that needs to be carefully considered, in the full understanding of all the drawbacks there might be. After all, the upheaval involved in retiring (which is often and very easily under-estimated until it actually hits) can be difficult enough in itself to adjust to, without pulling out most of the domestic roots as well. Ultimately, of course, it must be a matter of individual choice based on personal circumstances and temperament. There can be few rules. But there can be guidelines.

Type of home

If you are thinking in terms of moving, consider briefly the aspects of doing so which need, or rather

positively demand, forethought. Can you afford the
cost not merely of buying a new home, but of selling the
old one and moving out of it? How suitable will the
new home be in terms of its size, location, running costs,
convenience? Is it near to facilities like shops, a doctor,
entertainment? Are you sure you will not miss friends,
relatives, neighbours, and the many familiar aspects of
where you live now? How dependent will you be on a
car or other transport? Suitable as it is now, will it be
equally suitable in 10 or 20 years time? The 'dream
cottage' on the hill, for example, may be up a climb that
will be too steep for you at 80. Is the climate right, or
are you imagining it to be all the year round as you
have known it only during summer holidays? Even Italy
is cold in January, and there can be more rain in the
Mediterranean winter than on the British south coast.
Will you be able to pursue your interests? And, to be
severely practical, a couple should consider how the
surviving partner will be able to manage after the
death of the other. From that point of view, a house in
town near neighbours may be much more sensible
than a country cottage, even if less attractive.

Wherever it is, there are four main hazards against
which to guard in your retirement home. They are:
overwork, climbing, cold and isolation. A house that is
too large to manage and maintain, even if it is the home
you have lived in all your life, will become a growing
incubus. A garden that was a delight for its flowers,
shrubs and lawn, and a money-saver with its cabbages
and beans and fruit when you were 65, may be totally
beyond your capacity to care for when you are 85.

As for climbing, both hills and stairs which you can
take in your stride when you retire will probably make

you more 'puffed' as the years go by. There is a lot to be said, for that reason, for moving into a bungalow. If you much prefer a house, as many people do, put a handrail on the stairs and at the very least install a downstairs lavatory. Stairs are a menace to the elderly. Nearly half of all fatal accidents to women are caused by falling downstairs.

Warmth is going to matter more and more, too. In a large house, the costs of heating may prove beyond your means. If you are in an old house, or one that is not insulated or centrally heated, the cold will become an increasing burden.

The community

Finally, it is essential that you remain a part of the community. Even a self-sufficient person, preferring to be alone most of the time, will increasingly depend on easy access to shops, transport, medical attention and such useful facilities as the local library – not only for its books, but as a starting point for all kinds of practical help on matters as varied as rent rebates and chiropody. And if you go somewhere really distant, will you see enough of your children and grandchildren? Distant separation from them may leave you feeling lonely and homesick.

We have already seen the importance of planning in advance. With housing, this is more than mere prudence: it is a practical necessity. Buying and selling can take a long time, and for several kinds of accommodation, such as sheltered housing or bungalows in particularly favoured localities, waiting lists are long. And, of course, if there are many possibilities to consider, they will need to be looked at and discussed, and that can take

years. We have noted that often a couple will have
moved at the time they cease to need their family home,
probably well before retirement. Those who do not
fancy moving when they are in their 60s, still less when
they are even older, would clearly be well advised to
start thinking about their retirement homes as early as
their 50s. Later on, declining zeal and tighter finances
might hamper freedom of choice.

The first main option is to stay where you are. The
advantages are obvious – you know the neighbours and
the neighbourhood. You know the tradesmen and the
shops. You know your way around. You know the snags
of the locality. The house and garden are probably,
after years of effort, just as you want them – or if they
are not, they are, at any rate, 'home'.

But if the house still suits you at 65, will it suit you at
75, or 80? Are there stairs? Is it warm in winter? After
years of living in it, are there expensive items of maintenance which need attention? Can you afford major
improvements, redecoration work to deal with damp, rot
or woodworm, re-wiring, or roof repairs?

Buying, letting, renting

If the house is too large, it may be possible to let off
rooms. But that has many pitfalls. Tenants can be a
nuisance and an intrusion as well as a financial prop,
and often prove less of a financial prop 'net', than they
seemed they might be 'gross'. The house may need
conversion. Are you really up to the problems of being a
landlord?

Many do decide in their retirement to become 'landlords' in the sense that, perhaps rather informally, they
let off a room or two to 'paying guests', or, more formally,

divide the house into self-contained halves. Money spent on solicitors' advice on how to do this without subsiding into legal quicksand would be money well invested. It can be almost impossible to get rid of troublesome tenants (and tenants have a tendency to be troublesome). However, it is possible, though it is often a frustrating process, to get local authority grants towards the costs of conversion. If such work is done, be prepared for disruption, disturbance, delay and unforeseen expense. You may even have to move out for a time. Information on house renovation grants is published by the Department of the Environment. It varies from area to area, so should be checked in detail with the local authority, who have wide discretion in deciding how much help they will give. In times of their own straitened economic circumstances, they may prove rather unforthcoming.

A better possibility might be for the council to buy your home, convert it, and then allow you to remain as tenant. Or they may give you purpose-built accommodation elsewhere in the district.

If you are a council tenant already, then such problems will not really arise. You are almost certainly a priority client for suitable re-accommodation already. But if you are in privately rented accommodation, you will need to think well in advance about what you are going to do. What you have may remain suitable for your later years, but if not, it is important to consider the alternatives well beforehand. Private landlords are not usually in a position to be particularly helpful on this score, though if you live in a block of flats, it may be possible to transfer to the ground floor if you give adequate notice.

Living with relations

A further possibility is to stay in your house, even if it is too big, and invite relatives or friends to share. Here again, legal advice might be useful. However cordial the arrangements at the start, it is terribly easy for them to turn sour as time goes on, for all the many reasons that do lead to misunderstandings and difficulties in human relationships, particularly if money is involved. But apart from the finances, simply picture the possible complications each morning in the bathroom or each meal time in the kitchen.

Some retired people do succeed, however, in living most successfully with relatives – their grown-up children in many cases. They can either stay in their own home, or sell up and go to live with the younger generation. If you do this, you might be able to let your home instead of selling it but, again, this is something on which you should get legal advice. (As you should, incidentally, if you let a retirement home which you may have bought in anticipation of your retirement).

If your relatives do come to live with you, or you go to live with them, it is vital that you discuss matters thoroughly and frankly with them at the outset, or preferably before. There must be give and take, and real sharing of duties and responsibilities as well as of comforts. While the younger members must not patronize and mollycoddle the elder, the retired must not interfere. Everyone should be able to lead a normal life. No one should intrude on anyone else's privacy. While it does help if the different generations see eye-to-eye on most things, that is not essential. Arrangements can still work well, provided there is tolerance and, above all perhaps, a sense of humour. But as a rule, sharing of this

kind is not a good idea. The generations cannot help but
differ, and differ to the point of acerbity, over how to
run their lives, how to treat children, how to behave,
whom to have as friends. And if you go to live with one
son or daughter, there is a danger that this could be mis-
interpreted by the others, or lead to later misunderstandings. Unhappily, all is not necessarily sweetness
and light in family relationships.

It can, too, make a surprising difference on whether
you live with your son's family or your daughter's. If it
is the former, then a lot will depend on the personality
of your son's wife, for it is the wife who has the decisive
influence on family relationships within the home. Being
with your son's family will involve you in a close relationship with someone, your daughter-in-law, who has not
been a lifelong member of your family. If, however, you
live in your daughter's home, the relationship is already
established.

Where to move to

Moving to live with relatives could mean moving to
a completely new area. On the other hand, it may be
that you want to move to a different district not to live
with relations, but because you want a change of scene
for its own sake. And this clearly has attractions. Who,
after a lifetime in an industrial town or some unpre-
possessing suburb, would not be tempted by the thought
of a bungalow by the sea, a cottage in the country, or a
villa on the Mediterranean? Many people, after all,
live where they do only because their work obliges
them to do so. They may have been unable to move
earlier for all kinds of family reasons – one of the
commonest is the need to ensure continuity in the

children's schooling. By the time retirement is approaching, such reasons have usually disappeared.

Whatever the temptations, whatever the reasons for wanting to move, a decision to go must not be a mere matter of whim. It needs the most careful thought and planning. Whether to the country, the seaside, or abroad, a move should not be undertaken without thorough reconnoitering. It must be stated firmly that it is no good choosing a new place to live because it has seemed attractive when visited on holiday, or on occasional visits during the summer. Some seaside towns can be pretty dead in winter; picturesque villages can be cut off by snow; foreign idylls can prove to be disastrous on financial, social, cultural and climatic counts. Beware.

If you are determined to move – and none of this admonitory advice is to say that to do so is invariably wrong – it can be a good plan to buy your retirement home in advance. Over a period of years, it can serve perhaps as a holiday home, and can even possibly be let – though bear in mind the problems this can raise. Such an arrangement can provide time and perhaps money for any modifications that may need to be done.

But – where? There is much justifiable criticism in professional circles concerned with retirement and its problems, of the so-called 'Costa Geriatrica', the south coast resorts like Bournemouth, Hove, Worthing and the rest. So many retired people settle in such places that populations have become unbalanced, putting heavy strains on medical services and other facilities because of the preponderance of elderly people. It can be a big mistake to settle in these otherwise very attractive seaside towns if you are the sort of person who is young in spirit. And it can be wrong in just the other way, too – if you are likely to need more than the average amount of help from doctors and others. If you are 'young at heart', you may well find the 'Costa Geriatrica' depressing. If you are likely to need the regular assistance of the health or social services, or some other facility, you might find, for example, that hospital waiting lists are, literally, fatally long. In his play 'Sunset Across the Bay', already referred to, Alan Bennett's retired couple move to another stretch of 'geriatric coast', Morecambe. The man soon finds himself bored and complains that he cannot make new friends. 'Yes you can', his wife says: 'there's always time to strike out'. 'Not in Morecambe', comes the withering reply.

For all that, however, scoffing at the 'Costa Geriatrica', an unkind soubriquet, has perhaps been overdone. After all, the Eastbournes, Bexhills and Bognors of this world are places which are *geared*, at least to some extent, to the needs of the retired, and where even moderately outgoing folk should have no difficulty in finding companionship. And, as a small bonus thought, a home by the sea may be able to produce some extra income either if you let it when you are away, or take in paying guests, if you are the sort of person who can happily do so.

But the real way to settle the issue of where to move to is to make trial runs – going, if at all possible, at the least favourable times. Places which still seem attractive on cold, wet days are probably a good bet. In the years before retirement, you can make it a pleasant regular outing, even something of a hobby, to go in search of your retirement home, choosing a different place to visit each time until you have made the choice that seems best. But all the many factors that must go into the final decision should be reckoned with – proximity to relatives and old friends, financial constraints, facilities for health care and other forms of help. A wrong decision can blight your entire retirement.

If, on the other hand, your image of an ideal retirement home is somewhere not on the coast but in the country, 'away from it all', there are different possible drawbacks to consider. This is not intended to be a counsel of doom, merely a realistic appraisal of the possible circumstances that will, almost inescapably, have to be faced if they are to be surmounted. Will you miss friends and relations, or be near enough to see them regularly? Do you really want a life that is not only one of rustic charm, but is also miles from a cinema, a restaurant, a public library, or a chiropodist? The costs of country living can be higher than you might think, too. You may well be dependent on a car. Heating is likely to be more of a problem than in towns, because piped gas, the cheapest fuel, is rarely available in rural areas, while electricity and oil are expensive and solid fuel is inconvenient: it gets 'heavier' as you get older! Finally, in considering whether to retire to a country place, a man should realistically remember that his wife is likely to outlive him. Will the conditions be too arduous for her to cope with on her own, with no shops, neighbours or amenities near at hand?

Cost of moving

There is another aspect of moving that you cannot afford to overlook – the cost. Almost all the popular places to which people retire enjoy, if that is the word,

high house prices. You must reckon with the legal costs
and the expense of removal. Both will probably prove
much higher than you imagine, especially if you are
working on the basis of similar expenses as you recall
them from years before. The same applies to the cost of
new furnishings, unless you are lucky enough to take
over a house with curtains and carpets included.
Carpeting even a small house can cost several hundred
pounds nowadays, and curtains do not come cheaply
either. Further details of the financial aspects of accommodation are discussed in Chapter 4.

Some people want to return to the place where they
were born when they retire. Such a desire may have
nothing to do with whether the place has charm or
beauty. The urge is often irrational. But however
strong that urge may be, it needs to be as tempered with
commonsense as the desire to live somewhere that
seems attractive and sounds delightful. It is best to try a
place out rather than just go and have a look at it before
deciding to live there: after all, this is one of the most
crucial decisions you may ever have to make. Take
nothing for granted. Do not assume. Make sure there is
good local transport, for example. You can learn a lot of
down-to-earth information at the local pub. It may not
be the last word in reliability or supreme accuracy, but
local gossip can be extremely informative.

It does not make sense to move simply because it is
'the thing to do' when you retire. Research, however,
has shown that people do move on retirement simply
because they feel it is expected of them, and that they
would really have been quite happy to stay where they
were, even if it was a grimy, industrial area. Pulling up
roots in that way seems certain to cause lasting damage.

Building a new home

Consider, too, the possible difficulties of any house or home transfer. When buying a new place, be sure to get a surveyor's report. If 'doing up' a tumbledown cottage is what you have in mind – and this can be enormously satisfying despite the frustrations and hard work – assume that builders' estimates will *always* be exceeded by at least 25 per cent, and always get at least two written estimates. Make sure there is not a demolition order on the property and establish whether planning permission may be needed for alterations. It may be possible to get grants towards conversion work, but expect to have to wait a long time for decisions, and reckon also on the authorities being troublesomely insistent on details with which you would not have had to bother had you not approached them in the first place.

Building a new home, of course, can be the most exciting prospect of all. If you do it carefully, you can have a property exactly as you want it, subject only to the limits of your pocket and to building regulations. But, again, it will almost certainly cost more and take longer than either you or the builders expect. It is vital to be sure that you get a builder with a good reputation, and the *only* sure way to find that out is from other local people who speak well of him. It may be as well to hire an architect – then he can exercise continual, expert supervision from the planning stage to the last details of door furniture and other fittings.

For those contemplating a move, one of the best sources of information is *Parkers Property Price Guide*, often obtainable on bookstalls. The guide gives a detailed and up to date analysis of average prices, in every part of the country, of every type of accommodation from flats to large detached houses.

Legal aspects

On the legal side, selling one house and buying another is almost certainly going to cost several hundred pounds. As we have still failed in Britain to reform our antiquated and inefficient conveyancing system, the process is also likely to involve delay, worry and inconvenience.

Although solicitors have something akin to a closed shop in conveyancing (and, incidentally, take as much advantage of that as any trade union would) it is permissible for you to do your own conveyancing if you have patience and a capacity for handling detail. The work itself is tedious rather than difficult, and there are guides as to how it can be done. But leasehold and country properties can be awkward legally. It is unwise to do without qualified legal advice if a property is not registered at the Land Registry. Another problem of doing your own conveyancing is that the solicitors with whom you deal, representing the other party or parties to the transaction, tend to be rather 'awkward' with amateurs and, again like trade unionists, are not above 'working to rule'.

This applies, too, if you use one of the cut-price house conveyancing organizations instead of doing the job yourself or engaging a solicitor. These societies generally do an excellent job. They cost much less than solicitors and probably make fewer mistakes. But solicitors do their best to make problems for them, usually by 'stalling'. So allow a lot of time for completion of a transaction if using one of these bodies. Many people feel that, despite the high charges, it must be best to use a solicitor, but unless there are special factors involved this is not, surprisingly perhaps, the case. There are many people who have been badly advised, considerably inconvenienced and heavily charged for these privileges by solicitors without gaining any special advantages over the services provided by the cut-price conveyancers.

So far, we have considered the options open to those who own their homes. But there are many people who rent accommodation, and others whose present homes are tied to their work. Most employers who provide accommodation honour their responsibilities to staff when they retire, and ensure that they have somewhere to live. But not all do so. For people who know they will lose their homes on retirement, long-term advance planning is obviously essential. No one should delay in getting the advice of their bank manager, a reputable insurance company, a local authority housing department, or all three. Tenants should make sure they know from their landlord, either private or council, what their position will be after their retirement. If they go on a council list, they should check annually that they remain on it.

On the other hand, you may prefer to continue living in a rented home. This has the advantage of keeping any capital you may have liquid rather than tied up in a house. If you rent a service flat, you may avoid many of the worries of maintenance and looking after a garden. But, of course, this is an ever more expensive form of living, and there can be complications over tenancy agreements, leases and rent controls on which expert advice should be sought.

Sheltered housing

Another kind of retirement home that suits many comes under the head of 'sheltered housing'. This can take the form of specially-built small estates of bungalows or flats, or purpose-built communal homes, or even converted stately homes. All have someone on hand, like a warden or qualified nurse, to give assistance with daily problems as well as any emergency help that might be needed. Sheltered housing is provided by many local authorities and charities, mostly for those who are especially needy on grounds of either health or finance, and by private businesses for people who can afford their charges. For the better off, a new vogue is already proving popular in the United States and may spread to this country. This is what the Americans folksily call a 'senior citizens' community'. Again, this is a specially-built group of homes for the retired, conveniently sited and with all amenities laid on. Many may like this kind of set-up, provided it is not, as in America, a lucrative commercial gimmick designed more to benefit the developers than the inhabitants. But others might feel that joining a community that consists solely of people in the retired age group, with no children around, with perhaps not even pets allowed, would be more like putting one foot in the grave than anything else. Neither sheltered housing nor retirement communities are the same, of course, as the many kinds of residential home, because the people who live in them remain independent, with their own homes, their own furniture and possessions, and with the responsibility of organizing their own cooking and cleaning. Special accommodation of this kind is provided by a wide range of bodies, many of them known as housing societies.

There are hundreds, offering widely varying forms of accommodation on equally wide ranges of terms and conditions.

The demand for sheltered housing in its many forms far exceeds the supply. If the idea appeals, you should consider registering years before you are likely to want to move in. With such accommodation, you will probably have to buy a lease which provides a tenancy rather than outright ownership. This means you will lose any benefit from a rise in property values that you would gain by owning your own home, but you will be saved all the problems and costs of ownership, and have useful communal facilities into the bargain, like laundering.

Retiring abroad

Finally, there is 'abroad'. Moving to a foreign clime has strong attractions for the retired. The lure of sun and sea can be a strong pull after years of living under greyish British skies and through damp and chilly British winters. Many who have already retired abroad went because of lower living costs in places like Spain and Portugal. Others have become disillusioned with modern Britain and want to live in countries which they feel are more sensibly organized and governed.

Unfortunately, many who have gone abroad on retirement have ended up disappointed, disillusioned and poorer. The trouble is, there are so many aspects that can go wrong, so many ways in which you can be misled, or mislead yourself, into believing that the ideal retirement would be abroad. This is not to say it cannot work. But, and it is a big 'but', even more than moving into another locality in Britain, moving abroad must be considered dispassionately with the greatest care, in full knowledge of the many possible problems that can arise.

It is easy to take a fancy to a place while on holiday. But before settling on it as a place to retire to, consult the sunshine tables and other weather figures. Tourist offices provide them, and a selection is published by the *Daily Telegraph* each day. Of course, the weather is generally better anywhere in the Mediterranean area, or in South Africa or Australia, than it is in Britain. But it can be too hot, and nowhere is it invariably equable.

Nor is climate the most important aspect. Britain may not be an ideally-run country, but it has not undergone the political convulsions that, for example, have destroyed the homes of retired British people in Cyprus. Then, what about health facilities? There is a lot wrong with the National Health Service, and in a number of ways it is deteriorating, but it still provides a wide range of services, especially for those in their later years, which we forget about or probably do not even know about until we need them. Most countries to which people would like to retire do not provide either free or comprehensive medical care. Being ill in such places can make you bankrupt.

There can be social problems if you do not speak the language. There can be pension problems if there is no reciprocal pensions agreement: many British pensioners abroad have found to their chagrin that their benefits have not only been frozen at the level prevailing when they retired, but have been catastrophically cut in real terms by native cost-of-living increases combined with the falling power of the pound to buy foreign currency. Pension regulations are complex, and if you do eventually decide to retire abroad, you should check your position carefully with the Department of Health and Social Security before leaving.

There are many other financial complications which affect retired people who emigrate. There will be a lot of form-filling. There are tight regulations about transferring money abroad, on which your bank manager is the ideal person to give advice in the first instance. You cannot buy property abroad without approval from the Exchange Control Commission and the Bank of England. Furthermore, several countries lay down severe financial requirements for new residents. There can be heavy extra costs in transferring funds abroad because of the 'dollar premium', which can double the cost of buying foreign currency (not only dollars) or, to look at it another way, effectively halve your assets. There are, however, ways of avoiding the dollar premium in whole or in part. As only permanent buildings attract the premium, you can dodge it by buying a caravan on a site. Also, if a property has a British component, such as a British-made timber-framed house erected abroad, it may be possible to make part payment in sterling. It is also possible to use premium-free sterling to buy a property resold by a British owner. Finally, pensioners may be able to get special dispensation, if retiring abroad, to take out money free of premium. Or, you might be able to make an arrangement, through your bank, with someone in the country of your choice whose assets are frozen there.

If, however, you have the resources and resourcefulness to overcome such hurdles – and we have covered them only in outline here – and if you are sure that where you want to go will suit you – there are still other pitfalls of which it is best to be forewarned.

The advertisements of developers who offer, and sometimes depict, idealized retirement homes abroad, have produced far more sad stories than happy ones. Buying land and property abroad is usually a much more complex matter than in Britain. Can you cope with foreign property dealers, foreign legal systems, foreign architects, foreign builders? It is not a good idea to leave everything in the hands of some local 'agent' unless you are utterly sure that he is reputable. Very many of them claim to know their way round awkward regulations, or say they can 'fix' things. This is a sure route into deep, deep water with more than its share of 'sharks' in various guises. Developers who offer free trips to view investment properties usually show you only what they want you to see. It is better to investigate matters independently and come to your own conclusions without the benefit of the persuasive wiles of self-interested promoters.

If, despite everything, you manage to surmount all these problems, you will be joining thousands of British people who have retired to places like the Greek Islands, the Algarve, Malta and the Channel Islands before you. Despite revolutions, plummetting property values, ever high living costs, frozen pensions and all the rest of it, they stay on. Why? Well, for many, sunshine matters more than anything. But what else? Probably the same thing that keeps most retired people where they are – the difficulties of uprooting, of selling a home, and the fearsome problem of finding a new home, especially in inflation-hit Britain.

So, many retired 'Brits' stay abroad, too often forming sad and dispirited little communities, thrown in upon themselves, insulated and isolated from the local people on grounds of age, language and custom, living for cocktail time and the next round of bridge, bound by only one thing in common – a sense of loss and alienation. It is not a happy way to end one's days.

As was stressed earlier in this book, being older does not and should not mean that you cease to be contemporary. It is infinitely more difficult to be contemporary in a community of disillusioned expatriates. Those who live abroad when they retire must, if they are to succeed, be cultural chameleons, able to enter to a significant extent into the foreign communities to which they have moved. Otherwise, their retirement is almost certainly doomed to be a lonely waste of opportunity.

3

DOING WHAT YOU WANT

Wordsworth wrote that 'getting and spending, we lay waste our powers'. It was perhaps true 150 years ago, but it is true no longer. Today, most people retain their 'powers' long after their days of 'getting and spending'. Until retirement, it is true, 'getting' – work – is fundamental to life. Time is intimately linked with money. But that changes radically on retirement. Time spent need no longer depend closely on money earned, even in the case of retired people who continue working, unless they do so full-time. For most retired folk, life now provides unaccustomed leisure time. This creates opportunities for widening horizons, finding new pleasures, developing fresh interests, making new friends. Time is *not* any longer intimately linked with money, and is therefore unprecedentedly free to be used for different, though no less fulfilling, purposes.

That can be difficult, for one of the most rewarding aspects of full-time working life is the companionship of colleagues in the office, on the bench, or wherever it may be. Retirement means that contact of this kind is lost. So the temptation can be, with leisure time on one's hands, to keep returning to 'haunt' a former place of work.

That is a big error, not only embarrassing to those visited, but probably disconcerting to the retired person himself when he realizes that his presence is not wholly welcome. The occasional visit, of course, is fine. Everyone at work will be glad to see a former colleague who is flourishing in retirement. But no one will want to see a sad, old bore who does not know what to do with himself.

What is 'leisure'?

What does leisure in retirement really mean? It is not another word for relaxation. There will undoubtedly be more than enough time for taking things easy, but it hardly needs a chapter to be written on it! Few people can endure too much relaxation, as most of us know from practical experience – after a long holiday, we are probably quite ready to get back to work.

Then, too, there is packaged leisure, by which is meant leisure marketed in various commercial forms, from organized holidays to card games. These do have their place, and can obviously give enjoyment, but they are scarcely an adequate diet for an entire life-style. Simply 'filling in' the hours in an arbitrary, incoherent, purposeless, random, or passive fashion, is really to let others dictate to you, through the rules of games, the schedules of *Radio Times*, or the listings of the travel agents, how they want you to spend your leisure time. Real leisure is putting into effect plans you have laid for doing what you want to do. It is not doing what you have allowed yourself to be persuaded to do, let alone doing nothing at all.

To look at it another way: everyone knows, if not at first hand, how demoralizing it is to be on the dole. Retirement too is unemployment, of a kind, and the cure is the same as it is for those on the dole: occupation. In Chapter 5, we will consider both gainful and volun-

tary work opportunities that are open to the retired.
Here we examine the possibilities of leisure occupation.

Hobbies

Most people have had a lifelong hobby, or a lifelong
intention to pursue a hobby which they have never had
enough time for before. Retirement is an ideal time to
take that up in earnest. It is never as late as you may
think to make a start. The possibilities are almost
limitless, from bee-keeping to model railways, from
carpentry to writing, from walking in the countryside
to learning Russian. The clue to happy attainment in
almost any such activity is to find others with a like
interest rather than to pursue it on your own. This not
only helps to provide companions in retirement as
congenial as those you knew at work, but also enhances
enjoyment of the pursuit itself.

New skills

Learning new skills and developing new interests are
activities traditionally associated almost solely with the
young. But there is no reason at all why older people too
should not use their leisure actively and creatively by
taking up new pursuits. The brain does not shrink or
even significantly deteriorate because of age as such: it
can be used as fully in the retirement years as at any
other time. It is also wrong to assume that your memory
will almost inevitably fail as years go by. Some old
people become forgetful, but most, as a matter of fact,
do not. Certainly, a brain that is accustomed to 'exercise', that is kept in trim, fresh and alert and not left
to vegetate, has every chance of remaining healthy and
vigorous, and there is no reason why, for example, a

retired person should not undertake as taxing an activity as learning a new language. It is true that some people do suffer severe loss of recall, but this is usually due to the effects on the brain of extraneous physical factors – high blood pressure, perhaps, use of sleeping pills, chronic excess of alcohol. It is not necessarily true, either, that as you get older, you will be able to recall the past but not the present. If that happens, it is also due to the effects of extraneous factors, though not physical this time. The people to whom this happens concentrate, probably subconsciously, on the past, because they are sure that it was better than things are now. But if the present is good, as it can be even for the very old if approached in the right way, then awareness of the present can be as keen as any nostalgic recollection. Hankering after the past is a self-defeating pastime: even nostalgia is not what is was! While it is true that the ability of the brain to absorb new information and ideas does slow down a bit, the capacity remains as great and in some ways even increases with age. That is the important point, for time is no longer at a premium after retirement.

Educational opportunities

The educational opportunities that the retired find open to them these days are enormously rich and varied. They range all the way from broadening horizons in the reading room of your local library to taking a degree through the Open University – and that you can do even if you have no previous educational qualifications. But education in retirement need certainly not be confined to academic subjects. It can include the development of skills that you already possess, by attending day or evening classes, taking correspondence courses, studying books of instruction, following courses on radio or television, or picking up new ideas from others in local clubs and societies. You can find out about these at the library, town hall, or citizens' advice bureau. Most neighbourhoods have much more going on in this respect than we suspect. Every locality, too, has an adult education department, ready to help learners at any stage and of every age. Their courses are usually as enjoyable as they are stimulating. What matters is that you are an enthusiast for the subject. You do not have to be intellectually inclined to get a lot out of them.

The courses that local education authorities run are usually practical, on subjects like cookery, car maintenance, home crafts, keeping fit, painting, photography, typing, woodwork, and so on. But in the 20-odd towns and cities which are university centres, a much wider range is available too, covering almost every subject. Then, in addition to the Open University, in which long-term courses are done by correspondence, broadcasts, and at study centres and summer schools, there are the courses run by organizations like Townswomen's Guilds and the Workers' Educational Association (which is not, despite widespread belief, a sectarian body wedded to the Labour movement). Many WEA courses, which are open to all without qualification, place emphasis on class discussion and debate. They are strongest on topical subjects, often controversial, like mental health, industrial relations, the welfare state or African nationalism. These sessions can be most invigorating. It is no disadvantage to be able to join in these discussions as a retired person, with the advantage of age and experience. Indeed, the views you may hold

may be so out of date that they come as a breath of
fresh air to the younger students!

Learning a new language can be enjoyable and useful,
not only in itself, but as a route to other things. It is
not necessarily as tough a task as recollection may make
it seem to have been at school, because modern methods
tackle languages in quite a different way. Learning
another language can open the way to the understanding of other peoples, of unfamiliar cultures, of
different ways of life. It can be of practical use on
holiday, or even at home on occasion, should a translator
be needed, perhaps in a court, or at a local hospital in
an emergency, especially if you become proficient in a
language which is not widely known in Britain (and
most are not). Actually, one language which is extraordinarily neglected even in Britain is English itself.
Most British people have a vocabulary which many
foreigners can put to shame. Some of us use no more than
one or two per cent of the words in the dictionary.
Widening your knowledge of your own language, if you
are at all bookishly inclined, can be a fascinating
exercise, leading to deeper appreciation of what is
probably the world's greatest corpus of literature. It
could also help you to become a more effective con-
versationalist and even a relatively accomplished public
speaker – not a flashily erudite one, for no one wants
that, but a person who stands out for his command of
language and will be sought on that account. In a later
chapter we consider the possibilities of participating in
community affairs, such as local council work. An
ability to speak well in public will obviously help greatly
in such activity.

The prospect of strenuous intellectual exercise in later

life may seem daunting. But retirement is, in fact, the ideal time for it. It means that such education is being undertaken for its own sake, unhampered by ulterior vocational purposes.

It is as well to note that the Open University is open to adults whatever their age, whatever their previous education, and wherever they live. Residential courses, too, should not be forgotten. Information on these can be obtained from local authority education offices. Such courses are often the best form of study for adults, taking place in congenial surroundings, providing excellent opportunities for meeting like-minded people as well as others of the same generation but of different background.

Recreations

Many people have musical, artistic, literary or other creative talents which have remained dormant since schooldays. Retirement is an ideal time to foster them, and such pursuits need not be costly. They are activities which are as suited as any can be to the mature, more reflective temperament which tends to develop in later years as the impatience of youth fades out. They provide a fresh route to the renewal of personal identity, worth and achievement which can, in addition, give lasting pleasure to others. They can even, in some cases, produce a profit. Gardening is another activity which many retired people find enjoyable, and as long as it is not too physically taxing, it is undoubtedly beneficial.

A great range of activities is comprised in the term 'hobbies', and extends even further if we take in 'pastimes'. For almost every one of these, from stamp collecting to chess, from jigsaw puzzles to tennis, from furniture restoring to playing bingo, from amateur dramatics to numismatics, there are national associations, mostly with local branches, which can further your interest. They run into thousands. The starting point for inquiries is, again, your local library. Even if you cannot find the answer there to a specific query, you can almost certainly learn where the answer can be found. Another repository of basic facts is the *Daily Telegraph*'s information service.

A hobby may be more taxing mentally and physically than the work from which you have retired, but because you love it, it is no burden. Its value is that it refreshes the spirit, relaxes the body, dissipates the stress from which so much illness fundamentally springs. The ideal hobby is a preoccupation that is not ephemeral, but will be lasting, is something that will sustain you for many years and is more than a mere passing interest. Often, too, fulfilling hobbies lead to happy and satisfying friendships.

Besides special interest societies, there are clubs for specific age groups, such as the retired, and these are very popular. There are probably 10,000 or more such clubs, so there should be no trouble finding one wherever you may live. They are of many kinds, varying in their aims, the way they are organized, and the type of neighbourhood in which they are located. Some are day clubs, or day centres, providing a place where retired people can meet over a cup of tea or coffee, or perhaps lunch, join handicrafts activities, play a game of billiards or draughts or chess, attend a chiropodist, and so on. Such day centres are run in some places by local authorities, in others by voluntary bodies.

Then there is a whole range of clubs which meet at

less frequent intervals, from twice a week to once a
month or less. In many towns there are lunch or dinner
clubs, too.

One activity which can be a pleasant way of spending
leisure hours in retirement is motoring. In recent years,
particularly, this can hardly have been much of a
pleasure in normal working or off duty hours for those
not yet retired, but once you have retired, you can take
to the road at the least busy times. The chief problem
that driving presents in retirement is probably financial.
But if you can afford to run a car, there is not necessarily
any reason why you should give up driving after retirement. The older driver is often less of a risk on the road
than the younger, provided he is fit. The older driver has
experience. He is unlikely to speed. Such characteristics
more than make up for slower reactions. It is a myth to
think that older drivers meander indecisively. If they
do, it is not because they are old, but because it is in
their personality to do so, and they were certainly prone
to do it when they were younger. In the United States,
there are plenty of men and women in their 70s and 80s
who pilot their own aircraft, so there is every reason
why retired people in Britain, very few of whom could
afford that, should forget any qualms about driving for
as long as their sight and other faculties allow them to
enjoy it.

Sport

Sport, too, is a leisure activity which can continue to
give as much pleasure in retirement as in younger years,
both for the retired spectator and the retired participant.
Bowls and putting golf are by no means the only outdoor
activities left to the older generation. Tennis, for example,

is not so exhausting a game that it must be dropped: the experienced, wily player can invariably outwit a faster and stronger opponent. It would probably not be sensible to start some strenuous new activity from scratch at the age of 65 (though some very physically fit people have done just that); and while it might even be wise to drop some physically taxing sports and games, there is little reason for giving up such activities as swimming or cycling which can continue well into the 70s and beyond, at a pace suited to the individual. Digging the garden, sawing wood, painting a ceiling, or having sexual intercourse (as we shall consider in the chapter on health) are also strenuous activities which can be as normal a part of retired as of pre-retirement life. So, if *they* are all right, sport need not be excluded on grounds of 'age'. It is as well to continue reminding ourselves that 'age' is much more a question of attitude than of years.

Holidays

One leisure activity that might be thought to be all but ruled out by retirement, is holidays. The idea that holidays do not matter in retirement stems from the mistaken notion that retirement is one long holiday, and that, of course, it is not, if it is a properly organized retirement. During working life, holidays add a dimension to life and provide a chance to recharge batteries. It is no different in retirement except, perhaps, that opportunities are in one way greater, because there is more time available, and in another way smaller, because of financial limitations (though often not so much smaller as you fear).

The opportunities are greater because you are not

tied to school holidays or working commitments. This helps you to take advantage of out-of-season cost reductions. As travel nowadays has become a production line industry, there is much to be said for holidaying at unpopular times, when beaches are deserted, country lanes quiet, the staffs of hotels or other places of holiday accommodation better able to give personal attention. Some long-term package holiday prices out of season, specially intended for the retired, are now so low that a holiday need cost not much more than staying at home. These are not merely 'off-season' offers, but special long-stay, low-cost trips of two months or so. The disadvantage of these ultra-low price holidays is the risk of making a bad initial choice of a place to stay. This may not matter a lot on an ordinary holiday of a week or a fortnight, but it can spell disaster for a really long stay. It pays, therefore, to do some research beforehand. Make quite sure you find out all you can about what it is like where you propose to go. An unusually useful book for this, if you can get it, is the *Agents' Hotel Gazetteer for the Resorts of Europe*, which includes brutally frank assessments of named places.

Many British resorts make special allowances in prices for retired visitors, with 'senior citizen' concessions on entertainment and other facilities. The question of State and other benefits open to the retired will be discussed in the next chapter: suffice it to say here that you should forget any patronizing undertones in such terms as 'senior citizen' and do not be reluctant to take full advantage of such offers. They are an entitlement, and can be received by showing a pension book, or a card certifying your right to a State pension issued on request by the Social Security Department.

Travel

There are, too, concessionary travel facilities of several kinds, free bus passes in many areas, special rates for the retired on trains, some reductions in cross-Channel voyages, and cut-price excursions which are announced at railway stations. It is always worth asking at the town hall, information bureau, tourist office, or library of any place you are visiting for details of the facilities provided locally for people of retirement age.

As time is probably not a prime consideration, it becomes feasible to think of staying with friends or relatives in distant places you would never have been able to visit before. The chief drawback is the price of air fares, but, despite inflation, there are now many cheap flight arrangements run by the established airlines. There are also affinity organizations which can arrange individual flights at charter rates.

Travel agents have details of many other kinds of holiday, from tours of cathedral cities to fishing in Scotland, from staying on a farm to swapping your house with someone in, say, Bermuda. There are travel companies which specialize in holidays for the retired, offering a colourful variety of trips in Britain and on the Continent. Instead of a very long holiday, suggested above, you might prefer to think in terms of a rather short one, like a three-day cruise to Denmark and back, or a five-day tour of the Rhine Valley, or a week-end in Paris. The great thing about holidays in the retirement years is that the calendar does not matter any more.

This chapter may seem to have over-insisted that pottering around doing little or nothing, which has its place even in the most active of lives, should form no part of a healthy retirement, but that leisure even in retirement should be unremittingly active, unmercifully action-packed and 'purposeful'. Perish the thought! It is one of the many virtues of retirement that there is time to 'loaf' without having to feel guilty about it. But there is a difference between taking it easy and being idle. Idleness tends towards boredom, and boredom to degeneration. Retirement is an opportunity to do as you want, but only a fool would imagine that empty hours of fruitless leisure spell happiness.

With so much free time ahead of you on the day you retire, there will be ample time for lotus-eating. The leisure hours of retirement present an opportunity today that would have astonished the retired of even a generation ago and can truly add a whole new dimension to living.

4

THE MONEY SIDE

This guide has stressed repeatedly that retirement is a time of opportunity, potential and new horizons. But none of this is possible without money. Surveys have shown what everyone already knows (something that surveys are apt to do!) that what really worries most people who are approaching retirement, as well as those who have already retired, is not where they will live, what they will do, or even how they will adjust to a new kind of living, but, quite simply, how they will manage financially.

It is an unhappy fact that as things are, only a lucky few do not feel worse off after retirement. For many, the chance to develop new interests, to travel, and all the rest of it, is a cruel joke in their poverty. And even those who are relatively better off are often restricted by sheer shortage of cash. In Britain today, some 3 million of the nation's 9 million retired people have an income which is below the poverty line, despite more than 30 years of welfare state provision.

Our system of providing for the retirement years is confusing and haphazard. It has grown up in a way that has produced an almost incomprehensible and intricate set of rules and a bewildering variety of provision. The State pension, despite upratings, is a disgrace by international standards and still fails to provide financial security in later years for millions of people. Although a better scheme is starting in 1978, it will take 20 years to produce its full effect, as its funding steadily accumulates, and it will be at least ten years before it makes any significant contribution.

Besides the State pension, the present system is in part based on the private provision of occupational pensions. These, too, are complex and vary widely in their terms and conditions. Some are much more effective than others but, regrettably, all but a few of the best still lack several vital features.

Yet, although people say that it is money they most miss after stopping full-time work, a surprising number do in fact find that financial worries in retirement are less than they had expected. They manage quite well. The point is that the same applies to finances as to all other aspects of retirement: the secret of avoiding trouble is to plan ahead. On the money side, above all, long-term planning is of the essence.

We can assume, for example, that you want to enjoy a retirement income that is around two thirds of what you were earning. You want, also, to cushion that income against inflation. And a man will want to ensure that his widow will be adequately provided for.

Well, none of this can be secured overnight. Indeed, it would require years of careful financial planning, for requirements of that kind imply that in the course of a career lasting, say, 40 years, you must in one way or another put aside some seven years' or more of pay for retirement. It may seem impossible to consign nearly a quarter of your income into cold storage in this way, but it is essential if retirement income of that level is to be attained, especially in times of rampant inflation.

You may not wish to aim for such a high level of financial security in retirement but, actually, it is not as far-fetched or difficult as it sounds. It is important to appreciate that it can be done only if you start thinking and acting well before you retire. If you leave it until your late 50s or your 60s, there is very little that can be done to improve the financial prospects for your retirement.

For many, unhappily, it is not possible to provide in advance for retirement. We will consider how they too may be able to make the best of their situation.

It is not only because money buys food, clothing and other essentials that it is so vital to the retired. It also buys choice. Without some freedom of choice between different ways of spending money, just as with time, a fulfilling retirement is almost impossible. Choice is too severely restricted at present for millions of older people, trapped in the complexities of provision and squeezed unmercifully by inflation.

Planning income and determining a budget are therefore the most important aspects of preparation for retirement. You will need to find out what your pension entitlements are, how tax changes may affect you, what savings possibilities are open and how to optimize them, what outgoings you will have to allow for. All these factors imply decisions that must be made well before retirement is actually upon you. The time to review your financial position, in fact, is not later than a decade before you expect to retire, for this gives plenty of time to put right any major defects in your long-term financial strategy, yet is near enough to retirement for the calculations to be much more than merely academic.

State pensions

On the income side, there is, first, your State pension. The State retirement pension is now being uprated annually to keep pace with inflation (though it is nearly always behind the rising cost of living rather than ahead of it) and has stabilized for a married couple at the fairly low level of around a third of the national average wage. For a single person, it is about a quarter of the national average wage. At the time this guide went to press, the basic State pensions were £28 and £17.50 respectively. These pensions become payable at 65 for men and 60 for women. The age differentiation seems both unfair (why should women, who live longer, retire earlier?) and inflexible (why is there no provision for alternative retirement ages?) but the Government has set its face against any change on grounds of cost, so the rules are likely to remain for the foreseeable future.

The full pension is payable only if contributions over the years have come up to the required amount. If, for example, you have worked abroad for a while and did not continue paying contributions, this will probably cause a reduction in your State pension. It is important, too, to note that if you retire early, you do not become entitled to a State pension – though you might, through a legal quirk not yet ironed out, qualify for unemployment benefit. The contribution requirement, however, does not apply to women: if you are a woman who has not contributed, you still become entitled to your share of the married couple's pension, whatever your age, once your husband has reached 65 and has retired. A wife who is older than her husband must wait until he is 65 before she is pensionable, unless she has earned a pension in her own right through her own contributions.

So, to qualify for a State pension, you must be old enough and must have made the necessary contributions. But there is a third requirement: you must, also, have retired. The pension, in fact, is not, as commonly described, an 'old age pension'; it is a 'retirement pension'. This means that, to get it, you must have retired from full-time work. You can go on working without losing the pension, but it must be work that is not regarded as 'regular employment'. This is usually reckoned to be not more than 12 hours a week or so, or if more, then producing only a very modest income. You can, also, give up work and draw your pension and then change your mind and return to full-time work, relinquishing your pension at the same time until you are 70, when pension is payable whether you work or not. But you are allowed to change your mind on that score only once.

In part-time work which is not 'regular', and therefore does not affect your State pension, you can continue working for your former employer. But a break in employment of at least a few weeks at retirement time is advisable, for this establishes the fact of retirement from an official point of view. The basic point, though, is that you cannot continue in the same job, even at less money, or go into a different job that is full-time, and still qualify for the State pension. This applies broadly to the self-employed, too.

If you do carry on working, even if it is in a way that does not affect your pension entitlement, you may still be subject to the notorious earnings rule. This highly, and rightly, unpopular impost is now being phased out, but as matters stand, any earnings over £40 a week per person bring a deduction in pension, so that if earnings reach £59.50, the pension is extinguished and nothing at all is payable. It is a punitive tax, levied on earned but not unearned income, and is as powerful a disincentive to useful work as could have been devised. It is, in fact, a particularly cynical means of raising State revenue, or reducing State spending, but fortunately its days seem numbered. After 70 (65 for women), the earnings rule does not apply and you can have your full pension, even if you work.

Although you may be entitled to a pension, you must still claim it. This is quite easy. A claim form is sent automatically, or should be. The only thing to watch out for is if it does not come about four months before your qualifying birthday, in which case you should make inquiries at the local social security office.

You can get more than the basic pension if you carry on working without drawing it. Extra contributions while you work will enhance the pension by up to 20 per cent. You can also get a higher pension if your children are still of school age, or if you have other dependents. But the pension will be cut if you go into hospital for more than eight weeks.

The State pension is taxable. This does not necessarily mean that you pay tax on it because, for those of pensionable age, there are special tax allowances which mean that you have to earn well in excess of the pension for it to be included in the tax reckoning.

The State pension is payable almost anywhere in the world, but if you settle abroad, you will benefit from upratings only if you retire to a country with which there is a reciprocal pensions agreement. Surprisingly, this category does not include Australia, New Zealand, Canada or South Africa, although Spain and most

European countries in which retired Britons live are covered.

There are many other regulations affecting the State pension, for there are so many permutations and combinations of individual circumstance. It is impossible to do more here than give the guidelines, and specific queries should be taken up with social security offices. All too often, unfortunately, the local branches are badly briefed, and know nothing of rulings or changes in the regulations which have been announced in Parliament and published in the Press. So it is worth being insistent if you are sure of your ground, or asking to be referred to a higher level. Be armed, perhaps, with the relevant newspaper cutting. Quite often, local social security offices do not even have supplies of the latest available leaflets, issued free and frequently and in large numbers by the Social Security Department in London, to whom direct application may be made if you do not mind a delay in replying. Quite often, however, such literature is available at post offices, libraries and other centres as well as social security offices.

The basic State pension is only part of State provision. From 1961 to 1975 there was a graduated pension scheme to which most who were working in that period will have contributed. In terms of benefit to which their contributions will have entitled them, this was, not to put too fine a point on it, an actuarial swindle. It will produce only small additions to your flat rate pension. The maximum benefit which it was possible to accumulate over the full 14 years was £2.10 a week (£1.75 for women), and for most people it will be rather less. Your local social security office should be able to ascertain your entitlement.

A third component of the State scheme, this one earnings-related, will be introduced in 1978 and, should eventually ensure better State pensions than ever before. But those retiring in its early years will get only one twentieth of the full entitlement for each year they are in work after its inception. This means that if you retire in 1988, for instance, ten years after the new scheme begins, you will get ten twentieths, that is, one half, of the new earnings-related component of the pension. Whatever you draw will be an amount dependent on earnings subject to a minimum and a ceiling.

This third factor complicates prospective budgeting even further. On balance, it would be safest to reckon that, for the next few years at least, the total of these three components of the State pension will be to produce a basic pension of not much more than the present flat rate level, in real terms.

Private pensions

In addition, however, there are company or occupational schemes, to which millions of employees now belong. These pensions will provide the major part of retirement income for some 4 million public sector employees (many of whom enjoy the special privilege of inflation-proofed schemes) and 8 million other employees covered by schemes run by private concerns.

By the standards of other developed nations, most of these are mediocre. Only a few, operated by the biggest and most successful corporations, give good pensions and other benefits, such as widows' pensions. But improvements are being made, and employers are usually amenable to representation from staff to improve their schemes. It is a vital part of planning for your retirement to be aware of your occupational pension entitlement, which is really a part of your wage or salary that has been deferred, and to join your colleagues at as early a stage as possible in negotiating any necessary improvements.

There are three basic types of occupational scheme. The first pays a pension based on the average of salary throughout service with a company. The second is a money-purchase arrangement, with no guaranteed scale of benefits. Under this, what you get depends on what you have paid, the interest it has earned and the length of time it has been invested. The third, and commonest type of company scheme, is based on final salary, or the average of the final three or five years before retirement. Pension may be defined as a fraction of this, usually $\frac{1}{60}$th, in good firms $\frac{1}{50}$th but in many poorer schemes $\frac{1}{80}$th, for each year of service – so that with a good firm, 25 years' service will earn a pension equivalent to half final wage or salary, while under an inferior scheme, 40 years' service will be required to produce the same result.

There are many different rules applying to greatly differing schemes. Some make a deduction on account of the State pension, while others do not. Some include only basic salary, leaving bonuses, commission or occasional earnings out of account, whereas others, again, count them all in. It is essential to read and understand the rules of your company's scheme, wrapped up in gobbledygook though they may be. If you do not understand them, then it would be as well to get a clear explanation of your position from, perhaps, your trade union representative or direct from the pension fund manager.

Options

Because schemes vary so widely, it is impossible to generalize about them. But there are often options available under company schemes of which many employees are, at best, only hazily aware, and a careful reading of the rules may help you find one of which you can take advantage. It might be possible, for example, to make additional voluntary contributions in your last 10 or 15 years at work, to obtain a higher pension when you retire. To start paying such extra contributions only two or three years before retirement is unlikely to be of benefit. But paying extra over a longer time might help considerably, especially as contributions are liable to tax relief. Against this, such an investment is not flexible, for once committed to it, you are unlikely to be able to withdraw without heavy financial sacrifice.

Another common option in company schemes is the right to take some of the retirement benefit as a tax-free lump sum instead of pension. This widens the opportunity to shape the retirement income to particular needs, though there is an Inland Revenue limit on the size of sum you are allowed, of about $1\frac{1}{2}$ times final year's earnings if you have worked for a company for 20 years. But, of course, if a lump sum is taken, pension is reduced correspondingly, and a fairly complicated calculation is needed to establish whether or not it will pay to make the commutation. In most cases, it will, if only because the lump sum can probably be used to buy an annuity on the open market which is more than the amount of pension being lost. Although the annuity income will be taxable, like the pension, the tax rules are different, because the annuity is regarded by the Inland Revenue as an investment, part of which it treats as a return on capital and therefore not subject to tax. Although the remainder is treated as unearned income, and is therefore taxable at a higher rate, the net effect is likely to be in your favour.

Even so, this option must be exercised with great care. When you give up part of your pension for a lump sum, you may also be giving up a proportionate entitlement to any uprating that your firm might make to maintain the real value of its pensions. Or it might alter any widow's pension entitlement. Probably the best way of finding out whether the commutation terms your company offers are good or not is to ask a good insurance company to quote you the annuity they would provide for the lump sum you are being offered.

But there are other things, also, that can be done with the lump sum. You may want to buy a car, or to fit out a retirement home, or to take that long-promised cruise. On retirement, you may need your money for more mundane purposes, like replacing the old fridge or getting the house painted.

If you are retiring early, there may be special considerations to take into account. What are the conditions attached by your company's rules to early retirement? Does it depend on the agreement of the employer? Then, before deciding on early retirement, unless of course it is forced on you by ill health, in which case you may have little choice, check up on how much you will be entitled to. Those who retire early often find it is much less than they expect. The reason for this is that fewer contributions produce a lower pension, while at the same time the number of years over which the pension will be payable is greater. The effect is rather to multiply rather than to add those two factors, and retiring five years

early can cut a pension by as much as 50 per cent. Good
pension schemes will not unduly penalize an employee
who has to stop work for health reasons, but even they
will impose a deduction on account of contributions that
are not paid. Another point to bear in mind if retiring
early is that pension will be subject to inflation over a
longer than normal period. You will also be denying
yourself pay increases that might have come, if only as a
consequence of inflation, had you stayed at work and
on which your pension would have been based, so
again there is a multiplier effect. Finally, it should be
remembered that no State pension will be payable until
the minimum qualifying age, so you may have to
continue contributing into the State scheme to ensure
full entitlement when the State pension does become
payable. Early retirement is not, of course, the same as
withdrawing from a company scheme. If you do that,
assuming it is allowed under the rules, you carry on
working without contributions going in towards your
pension, and the pension you finally draw on retirement
will be reduced accordingly.

The rapid growth of occupational pension schemes in
recent years will help a growing number of people
entering retirement as the years go on. Even so, many
small employers cannot afford to operate them. Also,
inflation and the more stringent requirements for
occupational schemes under the 1978 'Better Pensions'
plan, are making it difficult or impossible for even big
companies to continue with them. Thus, many employees will not be covered by company pension schemes.
Obviously, also, such schemes do not help the self-
employed. Another serious weakness of most company
schemes is that they impose a heavy financial penalty

on the employee who moves to another concern. This usually means a big loss of entitlement. Finally, the occupational schemes are at the mercy of inflation. Even generous employers cannot offset high inflation and poor investment performance, and so cannot raise pensions at the rate necessary for their value to be maintained.

So if, when you weigh up all the components of likely pension income, you estimate that it will be insufficient, it is fortunate that you have done your calculations well ahead of time. This gives a chance for remedial action to be taken.

Saving and investment

Important Inland Revenue concessions allow you to save from earnings for retirement, and get tax relief in so doing, to top up your retirement income. Before deciding how to do this, you must weigh up your personal circumstances. Everything depends on your individual needs and means, how much time you have before retirement, what you hope to do once retired, what kinds of investment may or may not attract you, how much control you want over them, how secure you wish them to be, and so on.

The problem is made more difficult in a time of continuingly steep inflation, for money saved is money lost, even after interest gained, unless it is invested very well indeed. As far as possible, you must minimize the loss in purchasing power of savings or investments that you make. This means that as time goes on, the cash income you require will need to rise. But the higher the yield of an investment, the less of a hedge it is against inflation in the long term. So you need to strike a balance. You must try to estimate how much income you will need in total and how much will come from pensions and any other steady sources of income. The difference is the amount that will be needed from saved capital. The yield from that capital should not be more than five per cent or so if the capital is to be preserved as some protection against inflation. If you need more than five per cent, you must either lower your sights or consume your capital by buying an annuity.

We will consider annuities in a moment. If you have money to invest which you want to produce an income while maintaining your capital totally, or almost totally, an annuity is not the answer, because you lose capital by buying one. The most financially effective form of investment you can make depends in part on your personal tax position. That means calculations which take into account income tax, investment income surcharge, allowances for age and life assurance premiums, and other factors which change from person to person and may change from budget to budget.

You then have a choice of putting your money into the wide variety that is available of stocks and shares, or property bonds or fixed interest investments like government stock or local authority securities. For the small investor, security is all important, so the schemes run by the Government or by building societies are often most suitable. They do not fluctuate in value like shares, but the trouble is, that in times of inflation the capital does not appreciate, and even high interest rates do not offset inflation if it runs at more than ten per cent. The principal Government schemes are National Savings certificates, the National Savings investment account, British savings bonds and the Save As You Earn scheme.

Building societies also offer a variety of investment plans, tailored to suit circumstances and needs.

One of the more useful schemes, however, does help to defend the buying power of savings against the ravages of inflation. This is the index-linked Retirement Certificate, available only to those of pensionable age, to the maximum of £500 each. Its value rises in line with retail prices if held for more than one year, with a four per cent bonus if held for five years. This beats all forms of interest-yielding investment in times of inflation, particularly as the yield is free from all tax and is ignored for rent and rate rebate calculations.

For those who are able to invest more adventurously, there are many other types of saving. Unit trusts, for example, are funds in which investors pool their resources and put them under professional management for investment in the stock market and elsewhere. There are many kinds of unit trusts, with varying emphases on dividend income and capital appreciation, and differing too in the forms of investment they make. The most important point for the inexpert investor to remember is to buy units when the market is low. This is not the popular thing to do, but it makes sense, for the likely trend is up, which is to the investor's benefit in the long term. Buying when the market is high reduces the scope or likelihood of further rises.

Then there are the various types of managed bonds, equity bonds and property bonds, which are single premium life assurance policies which can be marketed like any other form of investment. The bond buys units in a fund set up by the insurance company with a stake in equities or property, or, in the case of managed bonds, in a combination of investments. Gilt-edged bonds are

another option and there are also guaranteed income
bonds, which provide temporary and deferred annuities.

There are, in addition, private banks and other
institutions which advertise widely and often offer
strikingly high rates of interest. Although they include
some reputable firms, they should be approached with
caution. The high interest rates derive from the fact that
the funds are used in high risk financing of hire purchase,
second mortgages and personal loans. Investing with
one of the big banks is secure enough, but as the interest
rates fluctuate considerably, income is never certain.
Loans to local authorities often bring attractive interest
rates, guaranteed for the loan period, but it is often not
possible to withdraw the capital sum invested until that
period expires.

Assurance

One of the best bets for the average person is endowment assurance, especially if it is taken out well in
advance. The top companies are much better than those
with the poorest records, so it pays to shop around. The
difficulty about doing so is that representatives of the
companies tend to blind prospective customers with
science, and make it impossible for the layman to
compare like with like. But a bank manager or insurance
broker can give valuable guidance, and the companies
with the best investment records are listed in the
financial press or city sections of the national press from
time to time. An orthodox with-profits policy can
produce very useful bonuses over a period, representing a
particularly healthy growth rate over a period of ten
years or more, especially as tax relief reduces the actual
cost. And, of course, life cover is provided too. Various

types of endowment policies are linked to unit trusts, shares or property, and these can produce an even better return, though the risk element is slightly greater in that the yield may be subject to fluctuating markets.

Finally, investing in a unit-linked savings plan might also be a good plan. This too attracts tax relief on premiums, of up to one sixth of income. From 1979, relief will be allowed on one sixth of income or £1500 a year, whichever is the greater, a concession which will help those on smaller incomes who need to save a lot in a hurry.

Those who do not belong to occupational pension schemes – this will include the self-employed, to whom quite different regulations apply – should save through a personal pensions plan. Such plans allow contributions of up to 15 per cent of income, with a maximum that is currently £3000 (but will probably rise in future years) which can be deducted from taxable income. This means that whatever the percentage rate of income tax to which you are liable, that same percentage of savings premiums is, in effect, paid by the Inland Revenue. By combining endowment assurance and personal savings of this kind, you can put aside a total of 31⅔ per cent of your income, and, for a change, get some aid from the tax man in doing so.

The trick, then, is to invest this so as to minimize the effects of inflation. If you are clever or fortunate, it may prove possible to offset inflation entirely. If you can keep pace with inflation, ten years' of saving will provide a fund worth more than three years' of earnings. With that, you can buy an annuity that will, for men retiring at 65, yield about half annual income.

Annuities

There are many types of annuity now offered by the insurance companies and other financial organizations and, as with so many other things financial, their variety is so bewildering and it is so difficult to compare like with like, that reliable professional advice should be sought. This need cost nothing: a bank manager or a broker will be happy to give his services (though doubtless in the hope of subsequent commission from business that results) and there are also a number of reliable and reputable broking and financial planning companies which can help. In the past, most annuities were at a fixed rate: for a lump sum, you bought a certain annual income for however long you lived. But inflation caught out many who were on these fixed incomes, causing considerable distress. To circumvent this, there are now all kinds of 'dynamic', 'escalating' and 'increasing' annuities in which the amounts paid out go up each year, in various ways and within varying limits. Naturally, such extra benefits have to be paid for, and therefore such annuities cost more. There are also annuities which guarantee to pay for a minimum number of years however long you live, and annuities which protect capital by guaranteeing to pay out a total equivalent to the original purchase price, even if the annuitant dies prematurely. There are, too, 'joint and survivor' annuities, in which payments are made to two people and continue until both have died. And there are other kinds, also, designed to meet any individual contingency.

Annuities are extremely useful and can produce a handy profit for those who exceed their life expectancy, for they continue paying until death supervenes. Their only real snag is that they are virtually irreversible and that they are at the mercy of changes in Treasury policy, but these are minor caveats. Companies whose terms seem exceptionally attractive should be regarded with caution. Are they reputable and adequately funded? The continuance of an annuity depends critically, unlike a State pension, on the financial stability of the concern that pays out the money month by month or year by year. (One assumes that the State will not actually go broke!) Annuities also limit the amount you might have wished to leave to descendants.

Annuities are not, of course, an ultimate hedge against inflation which is really excessive. But nor is anything else, except investment in such high risk commodities as antiques or coins, which is ill-advised except for experts. In times of high inflation, it is hard to know what to do for the best. Even in normal times, however, it is not easy to decide how to save and invest for retirement, because the imponderables are so numerous and the range of choices so great. As a general rule, one can only say, be circumspect. It is probably not a good idea to commit more than a half of one's savings to annuities, so as to retain funds that are more readily realizable. And the issuing company should be chosen with discretion.

Tax

A constantly recurring factor in discussion of pensions, savings, investment and income in retirement is: tax. It is another minefield. Eligibility for the age taxation allowance, which adds about 50 per cent to personal tax allowances, comes when either spouse is 65 (even though retirement age for women is 60 they become eligible for age allowance only at 65). But it is available in full only if total taxable income is below a certain ceiling (currently £3500). Above that level, the age allowance is progressively cut back until it is down again to the basic personal allowance. The effect of this can be punitive if income is £3500 or more from a job and, at the same time, you are drawing an occupational pension. For if the pension is raised, you will lose (at current rates of tax) 34 per cent of the extra in income tax. But you will also lose age allowance to the extent of whatever net pension increase remains. So the effect of, say, a £100 increase in pension could be that you would lose £34 of it in tax, and 34 per cent of the remaining £66, that is £22.44, making a total loss out of the £100 award of £56.44. Even though you will still pay less tax than if there were no age allowance at all, it does mean that you can fall into a fairly heavy tax bracket. The effect is made worse if there is 'unearned' income from investments. It can pay, in such circumstances, to switch to investments like National Savings or insurance bonds, which are wholly or partly tax-free. Just how and how much depends on circumstances. But as tax rates can rise to punitive heights on some slices of investment income, and quite moderate income at that, not the top level, it can save a good deal to obtain expert advice, so that taxable income is brought below the danger level, thus increasing disposable income.

Self-employment

We have tended to pass over so far the problem facing the many people who do not have any company pension scheme on which they can rely – some 2 million or more who are self-employed in their own businesses, or who are professional people like writers, lawyers, accountants and so on. They can take out retirement annuities, for which special concessions have been made in Finance Acts. Though intended primarily for them, such concessions are in fact open to anyone who has earnings which are not otherwise pensionable. For example, if your employer does not have a pension scheme, or if you joined the firm too late to enter its scheme, you are eligible to make personal provision, for which tax allowance will be granted. Even people who retire early from a pensionable job and undertake non-pensionable employment with the same employer, can start to build up a new pension themselves, despite having qualified for one already. And if you have earnings outside your pensionable employment, that too enables you to contribute towards a retirement annuity, within limits laid down by the tax authorities.

House reversion schemes

Because retired people do find it increasingly difficult to cope with inflation, many concerns now offer a way in which they can capitalize on the biggest financial asset they have, their own home. You may not wish to sell your home, but you can still derive an income from it, and without letting off rooms, either. Under various schemes, you continue living in your home, but a company will advance an amount up to around three quarters of their valuation of it. This is used rather like a lump sum to buy an annuity, providing a guaranteed income for life. The amount paid each year depends on how many years you can be expected to live – the greater your life expectancy, the less the annual payment. Some schemes guarantee payment after death to a surviving spouse.

Such income is subject to tax, but if it can be so arranged that most of each payment is tax-free repayment of capital, then the tax will not matter too much. On death, the original advance becomes repayable. The house remains part of your estate, though it may be necessary for your executors to sell it to repay the loan. It is not impossible to move house under such schemes, but adjustments would have to be made and some extra legal costs would be incurred. (In any case, as we have discussed in an earlier chapter, moving after retirement is something to be avoided, on the whole). The benefit is wholly yours if the house rises in value. If its value falls, this does not affect the income deriving from it, though when sold, the amount it fetches may be insufficient to defray the original loan. There is little likelihood these days of any substantial fall in the value of any property on which a hard-headed financial concern felt it was worthwhile lending money in the first place.

In a typical example of a house reversion scheme, a single man of 70 who got a £10,000 advance would draw about £520 a year for life. A man of 80 would draw about double this. A married couple in their late 70s could get an advance of £15,000, say, which would yield a gross £1845 annually. From this, tax would probably be deducted, because such schemes are heavily dependent on obtaining tax relief and so are really suitable only for those who pay tax. Also deducted from the gross £1845 would be interest on the £15,000 loan, which at current rates would take away almost all of the £1845 income. But, this is where the tax relief element comes in, there would be rebate on the interest payments. The net effect would be, if it were so arranged that income would continue to be paid out until both man and wife had died, that something like £600 or so would be received annually. Whether such schemes will continue to be feasible depends on the system of tax allowances, but it should always be possible in one way or another to capitalize on the value of one's house if it is paid for.

Such schemes are not the same, incidentally, as an arrangement which was once popular whereby a house would actually be sold to raise money to buy an annuity and was then rented back by the occupants at a nominal sum. That kind of arrangement had a lot of snags. It was inflexible, binding the owner to the house, whatever happened. It also denied the owner the advantage of any appreciation in the value of the house.

Financial hypothermia

One way or another, then, we see that retirement need not cause a kind of economic hypothermia, freezing finances at fatally low level. Intelligent planning, long-term saving, and income from work after retirement (considered more fully in the next chapter), can all help make retirement a time when a person may be hardly any worse off at all. For although income may not match pre-retirement earnings, outgoings will not be as high either. The mortgage will probably have been paid off. You are unlikely to have young children or anyone else who is financially dependent on you. There will not be the same commuting costs, and other costs associated with steady work. And there are many concessionary benefits, like cheap fares, low admission charges to cinemas and places like the London Zoo, cheap haircuts and other benefits which, though small, mount up and can make a significant total saving on spending. Retirement, then, need not be a time of penury. Indeed, some people can actually be better off. A married couple with husband earning the national average wage (about £64 a week) will have a pre-retirement net income, after tax, of around £45. A man who has been with the same firm for many years will find that his net State and company pensions come to a total which is greater than this. People on low incomes in their working years will often be no worse off in retirement. It is those who were on higher incomes who are most likely to feel the pinch, which is why this chapter has been devoted to ways of easing the pain.

Economies

There are still other ways of doing so. Retirement provides the time to find ways of beating inflation by, for example, shopping around for the cheapest groceries, taking advantage of special offers in a way that there might not have been time for before. A free bus pass, often available to retired people, will mean that no extra travelling costs offset any savings thus made. It might pay, before retirement, to undertake some basic re-equipment of your home with an eye to cost-cutting. Items which have got to the stage of needing expensive repair are probably best replaced. The capital cost of replacing electric with gas fires might well be a saving. Properly insulating your house, if it has not already had the hot water tank and roof-space lagged and the walls, if they are of cavity construction, foam-filled, will certainly pay for itself within only a few years (though double glazing will probably not).

There are other self-help economies, too. Ensure that you are on the most economical gas or electricity tariffs.

If the bills are too high for you to afford, contact the suppliers and explain your problem. Consider buying some household items wholesale, or from mail order catalogues, which can be cheaper than shops. Do not overeat – a way of wasting not only money but health. And remember that 'convenience foods', as well as often being the least nutritious, are also the most expensive. There are many cheap alternatives to the costlier foods, and vegetables grown in your own garden or on an allotment are certainly cheaper as well as fresher than those in the shops.

For all this, the fact remains that brighter financial prospects in retirement are open mostly to those who will be retiring some years from now, rather than those retiring very soon, or who have already retired. Millions of those already retired, those to whom the effectively patronizing term 'pensioners', emphasizing their economic plight, has been assigned, were never able to make proper financial provision for their retirement. For them, and many like them who are due to retire comparatively soon, there is only the State pension, in whole or part, and supplementary benefit, once known as 'National Assistance'.

Benefits

Supplementary benefit is available because the considered view of successive governments has been that everyone has a right to an income which keeps them from falling below the poverty line. There is nothing to be ashamed of in claiming supplementary benefit. No stigma need be attached to it. There are, indeed, scroungers who sponge on the system, but the vast majority who seek help are in genuine need. There are also, many in

genuine need who do not seek help. Many retired
people are too proud to take such benefits, which they
regard as 'handouts'. But they are not handouts: they
are a right. People who have spent the best part of their
lives working have earned that right. And the benefits
themselves are not given casually.

Retired people who fall below a certain level of income
can claim extra allowances of many different kinds,
worked out according to complex rules by social security
officers. Figures are constantly being changed in line
with inflation. In addition to supplementary benefit,
there are many other possible entitlements, covering rent
and rate rebates, special allowances for widows, the
over-80s and the disabled, the death grant, help with
medical costs, and various concessionary benefits. Full
lists of these, and details of each, are (or should be)
obtainable from your local security office. Some local
authorities, too, give help, such as television licences for
retired people who are housebound, telephones for
people in real need, or even holidays if seriously needed
for recuperation from illness or an operation.

The tragedy and absurdity of the pensions predicament
of many retired people who are suffering poverty is that
their plight has been caused at least in part by their own
thrift in earlier years. This is 'the poverty trap'. It arises
from the way in which basic pension, supplementary
benefit and the earnings rule interact. People below a
certain financial level lose on the swings what they gain
on the roundabouts: whatever they save for retirement is
lost in benefit entitlement, unless the saving is well above
average. It is true, of course, that many prefer to work to
earn, say, £15 a week extra, than not work and get that
amount anyway from 'the system'. But the fact remains

that about one half of all men of retirement age, and one third of all retired couples, have incomes which are below the poverty level. Whatever they do to get above it, they are penalized by loss of benefit, and so are kept below it. For people at that level, there is no point in contributing to occupational pension schemes, for their contributions merely reduce their benefit entitlement.

If you think you may be entitled to benefit and wish to apply for it, as it is your right to do, be prepared to undergo a means test and to negotiate an obstacle course of ifs and buts, qualifications and conditions, difficult forms and more difficult officialese. This is ostensibly designed to prevent scrounging. Unfortunately, it does not really deter scroungers, who learn the system and dedicate themselves to defeating it, but rather the many genuine applicants whose needs are real. The system is in fact designed to discourage claimants by confusing them and effectively ensures that the take-up rate is low, so saving money for the State. The worst affected are not scroungers, but the meek and needy.

Capital transfer tax

There are many people, of course, who are not that poor but whose means, still, are comparatively modest. Yet they often find, to their surprise and dismay, that being 'comfortably off', even if at the most modest level, brings them within range of such horrors as the infamous capital transfer tax, which replaced estate duty in 1975.

Under estate duty, it was important that anyone with financial resources above the average should consider planning for the disposition of their estate after death.

With capital transfer tax, it is not merely important; it is vital. For the key aspect of it is that the sooner planning begins, the greater the potential tax saving.

The tax is one of the most complex pieces of fiscal engineering ever introduced in Britain, perhaps anywhere. For the average person, one of its most important provisions is that it is no longer possible to escape tax, as it was possible to escape estate duty, by transferring a property at least seven years before death. Capital transfer tax applies to gifts made at any time, in life or on death. The rate at which the tax applies mounts cumulatively through life, with a final cumulation on death, and so, as you get older, the scale of tax on gifts or bequeathed property rises steadily from ten to 75 per cent, in successive slices. And, the more you give during life, the more you use slices of lower rates, and the higher the rate chargeable on death.

Fortunately, however, there are exemptions which will help most people. Nothing is chargeable on the first £25,000 of an estate left on death. Life assurance, wedding gifts of up to £5000 to a child or son or daughter-in-law, and up to £2500 for more distant descendants, are also allowed free of tax.

The most important exemption, however, is that of property transferred to a surviving spouse. On the face of it, all you have to do to avoid capital transfer tax entirely is to pass everything on to your spouse. But – there is nearly always a 'but'! – doing that would make it more likely that a greater aggregation of property would belong to the surviving spouse, so creating a larger estate, and when that surviving spouse died, the estate might then become liable to the higher brackets of capital transfer tax. In other words, although passing on all property to a spouse exempts it, at that time, from the tax, it nonetheless generally pays to pass something on to the next generation at each death, because the benefit of the lower scales of tax is obtained each time.

Just how much a difference it might make depends on circumstances, and the amounts involved. It can be a lot. To take what could be a typical middle class example, if a husband and wife each leave £35,000, the capital transfer tax will be, at current rates, (assuming there have been no previous chargeable transfers) £1250 each time, giving a total of £2500. But if the first partner dies, leaving all to the survivor, and paying no tax, the surviving spouse might leave a total of £60,000, and this would be subject to a tax of £7750. So it would certainly have been better not to have passed everything to the spouse at the time of the first death. The discrepancy will be even more punitive with bigger estates.

Other factors come into this, too. The bigger the age gap between spouses, the greater can be the benefit in deferring tax until the death of the survivor. The closer they are in age, the more they are likely to benefit by paying the tax in two stages. Also, the smaller the two estates, the more it pays to pass some on to the next generation at the time of the first death. For as the first £25,000 is exempt, *all* the tax can be avoided by dividing any estate of up to £50,000 equally. But an estate of £50,000 is liable to a charge of £4750.

Nor is this all. The ages of children who are beneficiaries of a will and the financial needs of a widow also need to be considered in deciding how to minimize the bite of capital transfer tax. It can help your widow considerably to give relatively substantial 'gifts' (as distinct from presents!) to your spouse during your lifetime. Then each spouse's will should give so much to the surviving spouse and so much to the children. It is all fearfully complicated. While the exemptions are probably enough to enable most people to escape the brunt of capital transfer tax, anyone with their own business or more than an average amount of assets should certainly seek specialist advice, and it can do no harm for others to do so too.

To sum up this, perhaps the most bewildering, aspect of retirement: think ahead, plan ahead, do the sums. Draw up a balance sheet perhaps ten years before retirement, and revise it periodically in line with the changing circumstances. On the credit side, before retirement there is money from employment, part-time employment perhaps, investments and other sources. After retirement, even if you carry on working part-time, you will lose your full-time money but gain income from one or more pensions. It may well be impossible to work out exactly what retirement income will be, but a little calculation will give a not too inaccurate idea. Then, list the outgoings: taxes, insurance, accommodation costs (including rates), maintenance, heat and light, rent or mortgage, new equipment, cleaning of carpets, curtains and upholstery. Then there is food and, doubtless, drink (and food for pets). Allow, perhaps, for some entertaining. Reckon up transport costs, spending on recreation like newspapers and magazines, books, holidays, television licence and maintenance, classes and courses, hobbies and sports, cinema and theatre. Include an allowance for personal spending on hairdressing, smoking, the football pools or the odd bet, charitable donations. And allow, too, for unforeseeable contingencies and miscellaneous items like Christmas cards, presents for grandchildren, stationery and postage. Sensible, prudent budgeting of this kind can be enormously helpful in preparing for retirement.

Wills

A final word on a subject many people prefer to forget about: making a will. There is nothing morbid about it: we all die. Many people foolishly put off making a will only to leave their surviving spouse, family and executors with a lot of unnecessary trouble, worry and expense. But there are simple will forms which can be bought at stationery shops. The basic wording of an ordinary will can be found in *Whitaker's Almanac* and other reference books, and the procedure to be followed, quite easy, is described. But care should be taken. A will can easily be made invalid, or can raise legal difficulties, if it is not properly, indeed meticulously, set out. Unless your will is very simple indeed, it is best to consult a solicitor – the cost will not be very great.

The point is, that you do not have to be rich to need to make a will. Anyway, most people are worth more than they think if all their possessions are taken into account.

The best time to make a will is when you are in full vigour and know clearly how you want your family, and perhaps some friends, to benefit from what you leave.

It is foolish to imagine that everything will 'sort out all right' if you do not leave a will. It will not. There will be ambiguity, uncertainty, and consequent ill-feeling. As there are strict legal rules about who gets your property if you die intestate, not making a will may well mean forcing your widow to share your estate with

your children, when none of them may wish to partici-
pate in a parcelling out operation of this kind. It could
leave your widow with a home, but no money. Making a
will avoids passing on a legacy of such anxiety. It can
prevent the unhappy business of having to sell treasured
possessions simply to settle family squabbles. It can
allow for such contingencies as your children dying
before you, or of you and your wife dying together in an
accident. It can ensure that those whom you love
receive what you would wish. It can see to it that there
is proper provision for death duty.

Shakespeare's 'seven ages of man' did not include
retirement. Having surveyed the field of finances in
retirement, one can understand why! It is no wonder
that money is the biggest cause of worry to the retired.
But there is no reason for despair, every reason to
prepare. Retirement may well not be an easy time
financially, but it can be a good deal easier for some
forethought, and a good deal less difficult than you fear.

5

WORK

A basic need

Any idea that the retired should work is still regarded as slightly outrageous. But retired people are no different from others in their basic needs, like health, dignity and money. Nothing happens on retirement to change those needs, unless it is to intensify them! The same applies to useful work: nothing happens on retirement to change the need for that either.

It is society's attitudes that condition people into the mistaken belief that they become radically different when they retire. So, society penalizes the retired, as we have seen in the last chapter. The earnings rule is only the most glaring example and, as such, is being shame-facedly phased out. But the fact remains that nothing more resembles retirement than going on the dole: the retired person is dismissed, deprived of his basic income, and all too often turned into an economic invalid.

But by becoming 60 or 65 years of age, a person does not become inactive, incapable or unintelligent. It does not make anyone less resourceful or healthy to move up from 59 or 64. Indeed, were usefulness the test, some would indeed retire to advantage at 50! But, and this is the point for our purpose, many, many more could carry on for years after 60 or 65. They should *not* be compelled to retire at the statutory pension age.

So, the best course open to many who face retirement is, in a sense, not to retire at all, but to work.

This is not just a matter of money, though there is nothing unworthy in acknowledging that money is important. But work is also a matter of using one's brains, and of purpose, vocation, self-value, fulfilment. Retirement into idleness or desuetude is a proven recipe for anxiety and unhappiness. Of course, there are many forms of routine work or drudgery which are far from fulfilling, and from which retirement is doubtless a welcome relief. But to move even from these into a vacuum could prove to be folly. It is not, either, a question of seeking to deny the retired the fruits of their retirement – the leisure, the new activities, extra recreation. But loss of job means not only loss of earnings – which can hurt, whatever preparation one might make – but also the loss of stimulus of work. That exists, often unrecognized, in even the most mundane of occupations, for it means having a place in an active community. Work, too, can provide status (however humble), give companionship and impart a sense of purpose.

Anyway, as thousands of people do not suddenly become incapable at the statutory retirement age, why on earth should they not continue doing something useful and productive? It is not as if Britain could afford to squander the willing and talented capacities of its most experienced citizens! During World War II, when those now approaching retirement were in their prime, people they then regarded as 'old' contributed very successfully in all kinds of ways to the war effort.

But in peacetime, employment policies for the retired seem awry and rigid, at both national and company level. While some people whose health has given way early on are virtually forced to continue in full-time work despite increasing inefficiency and absenteeism, others, the majority, have to finish before their natural stopping time. Economic considerations predominate, as they must, but humanitarian leavening of economic imperatives, taking the psychological and physiological needs of people into account, is badly needed and sadly lacking at present.

Danger of stultification

In a changing, highly technological age, the older generation understandably feels at a disadvantage. But the retired should never feel devalued by society's glorification of the new, the things that are thought 'best' because they are the most modern. That is to fall into the stereotyped role which society erroneously typecasts for them. Their need is to continue in contributory activity, and that is completely valid. Indeed, one of the lessons of the 1970s has been that the 'trendiness' which became such a cult in the '60s often fails, and that the values and approaches associated with older (and, by and large, wiser) people are often more durable, more worthwhile.

Retirement, too, is an admirable time for achievement, because achievement need not be impelled and distorted by ambition, or shaped solely to the requirements of an employer or a market. This is a major reason why retirement – which for many is a quarter or even a third of a lifetime – can be the most fulfilling period of all in life.

Work can be a splendid antidote to loneliness, which is a burden to so many retired people. It is vital to slough off the myths: people are not necessarily 'past it' at 70, 80 or even beyond. Apart from the Toscaninis, Shaws, Albert Schweitzers and Bertrand Russells of this world, lots of everyday people retain the ability to be useful to the end of their days. In many spheres, productivity is lower among the young, absenteeism higher, accidents and mental illness more common. If speed of response is less, it is at least equally compensated for by experience, as Jean Borotra showed at Wimbledon for nearly 40 years.

It is the stultification of not doing enough, or 'living down' to the negative expectations of the community, that makes older people act 'old'.

Avoid stress

This is not to exhort the retired to bustle around in 'purposeful' activity which they do not relish. As ours is an era of such rapid change that almost everyone suffers from some degree of 'future shock', no retired person can be expected, or should try, to be incessantly engaged in productive endeavour. But there is so much inherent satisfaction in having a job, if it is suitable, that work has to be a major consideration in every able-bodied person's retirement plans.

Paid or voluntary

There are, though, many factors to consider. There are the financial implications. You must decide where the work will be done: at home, or near to home? Or can you face commuting – remembering the expense? Do not ruin retirement by becoming a 'workaholic', so remember the other things that retirement allows you to enjoy and do not let work, however satisfying, become stressful. In retirement, work depends on your life-style, not, as before retirement, the other way round. Next to consider is the kind of work: what you did before, or something quite different? How badly you need the money will affect the decision. There is much to be said for the stimulus of something quite new – a different routine, a new workplace, new challenges. If money is not an object, then there is a whole range of voluntary work which can be undertaken and in which many people find the greatest satisfaction. Or you can do a bit of each, of course. But whatever the choice, it is always best if there is some commitment to someone else, otherwise, there is that fatal temptation to say: 'well, not today', and to slip then into a routine of idleness which gets ever more difficult to break.

Pitfalls

Although it may seem that all the ordinary avenues of getting employment – advertisements, employment bureaux, job centres – are as open to the retired as to anyone else, in practice this is not so. There are a few agencies specializing in placing people of 60 or over in jobs, but they are few and have not for the most part proved effective. Doing the rounds of the agencies can be as frustrating as it is for an author to receive only rejection slips in his mail. Large concerns with firm policies on enforcing retirement ages are unlikely to engage anyone who has already retired, even as a part-timer. Job Centres (the former Labour Exchanges) will not refuse to help, but they do not get more than a very few jobs for the over 60s. They have also found from experience that employers who use them are not usually interested in taking on older staff. Again, replying to advertisements which do not specify age is, almost certainly a waste of time. Hardly any employers who advertise a general vacancy will want to take on someone who is already pensionable: they are looking for someone who will stay a long time. And your own advertisements seeking work will entail expense and will probably bring nothing but letters from the get-rich-quick boys and loan sharks.

This must sound discouraging, but it is not meant to be so, and need not be. It is only to point out the approaches that are likely to prove fruitless. In fact, opportunities for part-time work for the retired have increased over the past two decades, despite rising unemployment. But in most cases, retired people get work through their own inquiries, persistence and, perhaps most important of all, preparation for retirement. Probably the most effective way to get work during retirement is to set about finding it beforehand.

Individual initiative

The best openings are among smaller businesses and organizations, often those that are not in a good position to make their requirements known widely but who recognize the value of an older worker's experience and reliability. The way to know about such positions is through personal contact, so it is individual initiative which is the most promising source of success.

Self-employment

But work in retirement need not only be for an employer. There are many avenues of self-employment. There are many small jobs around the house, for example, which can only be done at near-ruinous expense but which still have to be done and which a retired person might well find it both enjoyable and profitable to undertake. Anyone who is any good at being a handyman will find plenty of work in any neighbourhood, from papering a ceiling or mending a table leg to creosoting a fence.

So, a hobby could be developed in the last few years of full-time work to provide a part-time job in retirement. But it need not be done that way. The essential point is that it is in those final years of full-time work that the ground should be laid. The opportunities should be looked at, the approaches made, the contacts established. Everyone – bank manager, colleagues, friends at work or at the club, neighbours – should all know you are on the look-out. It is much easier to secure post-retirement work in this way, before actually retiring, than to start a long haul afterwards towards finding something.

Some professional people can set up as consultants and do as well after retirement as before. Those in such specialities as engineering, public relations, management, accountancy and so on, often find there is more than enough for them to do. But even apart from that, the scope of employment really is as wide for the retired as for those of any age. To list all the opportunities would be impossible, and to instance some would merely be to give an arbitrary selection. Almost any hobby can be turned into a business one way or another: photography, flower arranging, making furniture, for example, though before embarking on a venture be sure there is a market for the product or service being offered. Many other interests, too, can be turned to good financial account. Every neighbourhood needs its part-time teachers, secretaries and office assistants, pedestrian-crossing keepers, dental receptionists, relief librarians, car park attendants and other helpers of every kind.

Many people approaching retirement think they would fancy running a pub, perhaps, or some kind of shop like a newsagents or fancy goods store. Unless there are special circumstances, this is not to be recommended. Such work can be both tying and tiring. It needs a lot of investment in both time and money. It can involve much worry. And, for some unexplained reason, the whole trend of recent Government financial policy has been to put the squeeze on such self-employed people. Hard work harms no-one, not even in retirement, but there are limits, and those limits probably have to be exceeded, as far as the retired are concerned, in work of this kind.

The retired should also be wary of concerns which offer work to be done at home – more often to women than men, things like addressing envelopes or sewing soft toys. The rates of pay are usually abysmally low, so low, in fact, that official efforts are being made to stop the racket. The retired should also avoid any involvement with 'franchise' outfits, usually involving a capital outlay. Even those which are honest require more work than any retired person ought to take on.

Two final things to watch for if undertaking paid work – small details but possibly important. Running any business, even being a freelance writer or artist, almost certainly means tangling with V.A.T., which entails more book-keeping and dealings with the bureaucracy than you may wish to handle. The other is the possibility of crossing some trade union or other by undertaking part-time work. Smaller firms are less concerned in general with 'closed shops' and union sensibilities than large ones.

Community service

If you are in the happy position of not needing to supplement your retirement income, or have plenty of time left over after a part-time job, there is a wide range of voluntary work open to you. This can be the happiest and most interesting of all, provided it is taken on with genuine enthusiasm and does not become an unwelcome burden.

It often happens that when people know that someone is about to retire, they approach him to become chairman of this committee or organizer of that appeal, or whatever. Never feel obliged to undertake such commitments if you do not really want to do so, for a willing horse will be unashamedly exploited. Avoid, also, taking on important sounding posts just to enhance a sense of power or position. Such work can bring all the anxiety, hard work and stress of a demanding pre-retirement career. The rivalry and backstabbing on the committees of voluntary bodies can be just as vicious as in the boardrooms of industry. Instead, there is plenty of scope for voluntary work that brings more contentment, and is no less satisfying, at humbler levels. In retirement, no one needs to prove himself. As that is one of the joys of older age, make the most of it.

Another thing to recognize is that not everyone is suited to voluntary work. It usually requires some concern for the community, some dedication or compassion, a certain selflessness on behalf of some special section, usually disadvantaged in some way. It is particularly important to be good at getting on with others, no matter how different from yourself they may be, for voluntary work draws hardly any class, social, educational or economic distinctions in its recruiting.

That said, the range open is almost limitless. There are those who act as voluntary drivers for hospital out-patients – their driving expenses are refunded but they give their time free. Others work for the 'Samaritans', the organization which helps people in despair and has saved many from suicide, or for 'Meals on Wheels'. Nearly every neighbourhood has its associations, from writers' circles to rambling clubs, which need someone behind the scenes to balance the books, check the membership lists, send out notices, keep the wheels oiled. There is certainly no shortage of voluntary work, much needed and appreciated, in any community.

Local government

One of the most useful ways in which any retired person with some special experience can serve the community is by getting elected to the local council. Local government touches on many aspects of life, often crucially. The bigger authorities have many com-mittees which oversee such matters as libraries, transport, public health, spending, the social services, and this work demands a lot of time and attention. It is ideally suited to the alert retired person, who does not need to worry too much about the amount of time it takes up.

There can be some expense in local council service, though it is usually reimbursed. Unfortunately, just to make life a little more difficult than it need be, the National Insurance Commissioners have decided that attendance allowances paid to councillors can count as gainful remuneration, and so in at least one case have stopped payment of the State retirement pension to a councillor and his wife. The attendance allowance in question was unusually high, so the decision may not apply in every instance, but it is something to watch for.

Obviously, however, voluntary work need not only be of a formal kind. An Age Concern survey in 1975 found that many of those who worked for charities and organizations enjoyed higher than average incomes, but those below the average tended to do their voluntary work in the form of helping each other out. That is just as valid, useful, and fulfilling. What the survey did make clear was that most retired people who do voluntary work attest readily to the considerable satisfaction they derive from it. There, perhaps, is a lesson not only for those embarking on retirement, but for everyone.

The survey also gave interesting examples of the work people did before retirement and after. A chairman of a bank took up an unpaid directorship – a fairly obvious transition, perhaps. But the chief engineer of a local authority became the treasurer for two local groups, a research chemist undertook church work, a coach builder worked for St. John's Ambulance, while a store manager did charitable work through his Rotary Club. Among women, one who had been a teacher did recordings for the blind, a secretary did hospital visiting, a home helper worked for the Citizens Advice Bureau and the manageress of an employment agency did Red Cross and WRVS work.

A tonic

The moral of this chapter, perhaps, is this: there is immense value in work, beyond the financial, and a retirement without at least some work is a life without some of its spice. Work need not be the antithesis of pleasure, as so many believe, and it is a poor commentary on our educational and economic system that so many people do hate the work they do. Is this not one reason for strikes? Retirement provides a more legitimate chance to escape from such boredom and frustration for those unlucky enough to have endured them, while giving a new lease of stimulation to those who have found their work enjoyable. People whose work is satisfying do not watch the clock, or even think about it, and are often loath to take a break even for food or sleep. They do not tire as easily as others, either each evening or as the years go by. Those who live longest often turn out to be people who have worked hardest and most fulfillingly. There is, surely, some significance in the fact that so many of those who most pour themselves into their work – musicians and conductors, artists and inventors, very often live to great ages and continue to be active in their work until almost their dying hours. Verdi composed much of his greatest work in his 8os, Titian was still painting masterpieces at 98. They never 'retired', and the point about them was that they were *not* exceptional in the sense that they were men of exceptional energy (though obviously they were of exceptional genius). It is not so much that unusual reserves of energy enable men like them to go on working, but the other way round – the inspiration and satisfaction of the work creates the reserves of energy. Many people reach their peak, or are still at it, just at the time when they are forced to retire. It is senseless if they give up there and then, simply because they have crossed some wholly notional chronological Rubicon laid down by the Social Security Acts. Those who remain actively engaged do not go to seed, but thrive. Work, rightly chosen, is a veritable tonic.

6

KEEPING AGE AT BAY

Health in retirement

Entering retirement means that you are growing old. There is no getting away from that. But getting older does not, repeat not, make it inevitable that illness and disability, or aches, pains and severer pains, let alone advancing senility and loss of virility, are to be your lot in life. Sweeping generalizations are unwise, but if there is one that is true, it is this: it is perfectly possible for very many retired people to remain healthy, fit, active and well to the end of their days.

Many diseases associated with ageing are not caused by being old. They have much earlier beginnings, but because they take years to become manifest, they are identified with being older. And because they have earlier beginnings, it is possible to do something about them early. Until recently, only 'quacks' attributed most bodily ills to diet, bad habits and wrong living, but today this has become almost a truism of orthodox medicine. Those who smoke or drink to excess, who overeat, who take no exercise, do not generally die in middle age. They live on to retirement, and then the effects of their earlier habits begin to show.

Conditions like cataract and diabetes are usually considered 'diseases of age' but they usually build up over a time and are often correctable or avoidable in the 30s,

40s and 50s. Even arthritis is not an old person's disease:
it is found among children, too. Much can be done to
prevent even those most dreaded conditions, heart
attack and cancer.

Of course, no one can prevent the onset of age. But
let us be rid of any notion that going into retirement of
itself means acquiring some new medical status. As
people age, so their health becomes more vulnerable.
But a lot can be done to minimize this.

Age not the problem

The physical changes of old age, in fact, are almost
trifling compared with the handicaps imposed on old
people by society and convention. A major cause of
illness among the retired is not any inbuilt physical
decline, but degeneration encouraged by lack of activity
and boredom. A vital factor in mental and physical
health is attitude: those who expect to be infirm will
usually become infirm. Those who strive to remain fit
stand by far the best chance of retaining their vigour.

It is important to get away from conventional notions
of 'old people'. After all, there are bald men of 30 and
hairy men of 80. There are centenarians whose minds
are fresh and alert, yet many a young dullard. Little is
known about what causes the ageing process to develop
more rapidly in some than others – probably among the
many things that come into it are genetic inheritance,
living and working conditions throughout life, psychological disposition, individual habits and outlook.
But while we can do nothing to prevent changes in every
part of the body as the years go by, we can do much to
ameliorate their effects and to maximize the potential
of mind and body that we possess.

This does not mean having to adopt whatever is the fashionable dietary fad, or insisting that everyone must adopt the same routine, like jogging round the nearest park each day. It *is* a matter of seeing health and ageing in the round, as a process that begins when life itself begins, that can already be noticeable in youth, is usually obvious by early middle age, yet can be coped with very happily by most people well into their advancing years. Not everything about ageing is satisfactory, but the process is far from intolerable if one does not give in to it.

That the right attitude is a vital part of keeping healthy was a point made in the last chapter. Keeping busy is a tonic in itself, and those who have nothing to do, often become so pre-occupied with health, to the point of hypochondria, that they actually generate their own illness. People who do not expect to be ill will more often than not avoid illness, if they take proper care of themselves. The important thing is to get on with the business of living.

But if older age is a continuation of active life, and *not* a qualitatively different stage dominated by disability, changes still do occur. Long sight develops, hearing and the sense of smell decline. Lung capacity decreases and the heart grows less able to take exertion, though it normally remains, and can be helped to remain, surprisingly strong. Changes in the bones, joints and muscles reduce mobility. Nearly all the processes of the body slow down, and this affects everything from the skin, which becomes less taut and less able to retain warmth, to the replacement of cells to offset the wear and tear on internal organs. But none of this is anything to be alarmed about. For a person retiring at 65, the process has already been going on throughout working life. Anyone who has led a healthy life until retirement should clearly continue to do so and will have every expectation of remaining well. Anyone who has been less careful will need to face the possibility that their retirement years may become years of illness, and acknowledge that the time has come to adopt precautionary habits.

It is unwise to generalize about health, because people vary so widely, and the range of their tolerance is enormous. Every elderly person has his recipe for a healthy long life, and almost all break the rules in one way or another. But there is at least one fundamental truth: thin people live longer than fat people. This leads us immediately to the question of nutrition.

Sensible eating

Middle-age spread is not a disease of middle age but of social custom or individual bad habit, and obesity at any age is a health hazard which is almost always avoidable. In later years, it can be a killer. Not all overweight people die prematurely, of course, but there is no doubt that fat puts extra strain upon the heart. Excessive intake of fats and sugars clogs the arteries. A diet without roughage harms the bowels and toxifies the system. In short, a person must be well nourished to be healthy, too much is as bad as too little, and the body is only as sound as the ingredients which go into its making and maintenance.

Food is one of life's pleasures. Retirement is not a time to be a killjoy. But the foundations of obesity, and many other nutritionally derived conditions, are laid earlier on in life, so it is with health as with other aspects of retirement – much can be done by way of preparation. There is no need to change diet in retirement, unless the diet before was an unhealthy one. Calorie intake does not need to be as high as before if less energy is being used, as will probably become the case in the later years – if not immediately after retiring. Diet should be mixed and balanced, and should include either fresh fruit and vegetables or at the very least, if these are not acceptable, fruit syrups like rosehip or blackcurrant. Vitamin pills and other 'elixirs' will do little harm, but can do no more than a proper food intake and are far more expensive.

The body also needs liquid, but alcohol and artificially sweetened soft drinks in excess can be as bad as butter or biscuits.

This is, perhaps, a counsel of nutritional perfection. A little of what you fancy, if theoretically harmful, will probably do you a little good – provided it is only a *little* of what you fancy. And because preparing an ideally balanced diet can be a bother, many retired people prefer convenience meals that can be easily cooked. But these are usually expensive and should only really be used as an occasional extravagance, or in some kind of emergency. An excellent 'convenience' food from a nutritional standpoint, by the way, is shop-bought fish and chips.

Apart from costs, the main problem which often faces the retired is the trouble of preparing meals for only two people, or only one in many cases. It could be well worth attending a short local cookery course. Alternatively, a Penguin book by Louise Davies called *Easy Cooking for One or Two* is a handy guide; and there are others.

As for value for money, milk is one of the best foods going. It can be used in many ways, is always available, and is still comparatively cheap. Cheese and yogurt are also nutritious, but butter, except in very moderate amounts, should be avoided because of its high cholesterol content. Polyunsaturated margarines are much better from a health point of view. Eggs, milk and fish are better sources of protein than meat for those getting on in years.

Dental care

Fundamental to nutrition are good teeth, preferably the natural ones, but if not, dentures that fit well. Teeth start the vital process of breaking down foods and without them either the stomach will have too much digesting to do, causing indigestion, or pulped or soft food will be taken which does not need much chewing and which is therefore likely to be nutritionally deficient.

Teeth are worth keeping and worth caring for. A regular visit to the dentist is essential and can not only save a lot of pain but has beneficial side effects on many other aspects of health. Surprisingly few people know how to keep their teeth and gums really clean or healthy, and in later years the consequences are much more manifold than bad breath. Simple brushing with a toothbrush and toothpaste, even after every meal, is not enough in later years, and keeping the spaces between the teeth clear of plaque, with dental floss or specially designed toothpicks, becomes important. A dentist can show you how to maintain a high standard of oral hygiene and do the regular maintenance that keeps the teeth in trim.

Those who wear dentures should keep them scrupulously clean and not fall into the temptation of taking dentures out if they are uncomfortable, for this makes them more difficult to get used to. If discomfort persists, then the dentures probably need adjustment by the dentist. Well-fitting dentures will be comfortable after a while, if not at first, and are much more efficient and natural looking nowadays than they used to be. They are as good for morale as for nutrition, improving both looks and clarity of speech.

Keeping fit

Apart from nutrition, the other basic ingredient of keeping healthy in retirement is exercise.

Of course, the strenuous games of youth are out, and it would be folly for anyone to over-exert themselves. But many elderly people do keep up such beneficial activities as cycling, swimming and dancing. Golf or just walking the dog are good too. The important thing is to keep limbs and muscles active. As time goes on, the joints do tend to creak and ache a bit, but the remedy for that is generally not to take it easy (unless specially advised by the doctor), but to exercise more. Studies have proved that the more active people are in their later years, the less operations and other hospital care they need, and the longer they tend to live. Of course, a long life wracked with pain and illness is not what anyone would want for the sake of piling up the years, but good health does not come in separate compartments – the person who is physically active is more likely to be healthy in other ways too, just as the person on a good diet is more likely to want to be physically active.

Mere 'exercise' – physical jerks before breakfast, routine jogging, a walk round the block taken out of a sense of duty rather than for the pleasure of it – is a somewhat joyless, soul-destroying way of keeping fit. Fat men trying to work off their excesses in gymnasiums by lifting weights and pedalling stationary cycles are a poor advertisement for exercise. Much better is the exercise that arises naturally, the kind that hill farmers and others who work in the open air get quite spontaneously. 'Civilization', however, puts most of us behind desks, steering wheels or machine tools of one kind or another, and so we do need to create artificial forms of exercise. But let them be pleasurable, like golf or dancing. Also, sudden spurts of exertion can be worse than useless. The really unfit should start gradually, after taking medical advice. Once they have attained a reasonable level of fitness, they can keep it up by adopting a life style into which it can be integrated, perhaps by taking on a job within walking distance, not too near and not too far.

Sex

Another form of physical activity is sex. It can, and should, have its place in the life of the retired. Most people assume they will lose a desire or capacity for sex in later years, just as they are resigned to losing their teeth. They are wrong on both counts. While performance does decline, especially among men, the *belief* that potency wanes is a much stronger anti-aphrodisiac than the actual physical changes that occur.

There is nothing innately indecent or immoral in lovemaking after 60, or after 90 for that matter. The sexual urges are no more subject to the statutory retirement rules than the lungs or the digestion. Anyway, sex is more than intercourse. The expression of affection is the healthiest feature of any relationship. As with other aspects of health, there are no 'norms': some in their 70s continue to enjoy intercourse several times a week; others have a less frequent pattern, almost certainly in line with their activity earlier in life.

There are probably more myths surrounding sex than any other aspect of human life, and one of them is that the old do not need it and do not want it. The fact is that the sex drive is almost lifelong. It is only convention and the embarrassments bred by social attitudes that have disguised this biological fact. Impotence in men, after retirement as before it, is more in the mind than the body, and anxiety about performance can destroy it. Women as well as men can continue to need and enjoy full sexual satisfaction into their 70s and even 80s. Relief from the strains of work and a career may even mean that retirement brings an increase in sexual activity. This is physically beneficial and does not, contrary to legend, put a strain on the heart or encourage strokes.

Some older men experience trouble with the prostate gland, and this may sometimes have to be removed. Prostatectomy is a much safer and simpler operation than it once was, and although it causes sterility, that is, the inability to father children, it does not bring impotence, that is, the inability to have intercourse.

Doctors
This leads to an important point about medical help in general. Many retired people mistakenly assume that their aches, illnesses and disabilities are part of the

ageing process, and that therefore nothing much can be done to alleviate them. This is not so. Many conditions which afflict those getting on in years can be eased and can be cured. Indeed, they do not have anything to do with age at all.

So, while much can be done by way of prudent self-help, sensible self-care and intelligent self-treatment for minor conditions, no one should hold back from seeking medical help when necessary. The National Health Service, despite its many failings, does still provide, along with the personal social services, a wide range of comprehensive care of every kind, from acute surgery and major operations to chiropody clinics, denture adjustment, and many forms of remedial therapy and other treatments. Those who subscribe to private provident schemes for medical care can be sure not only of comprehensive care, but quick provision of it in rather more salubrious surroundings than the NHS usually gives. Anyone who can afford private medical insurance should take it out well before retirement, when premiums are lower, rather than leave it to later, when an age bar might operate or exclusion clauses might make it hardly worthwhile.

But whether through the State system or privately, regular check-ups are important. No one should feel inhibited about seeing their doctor for advice or about anything to do with their health that is worrying them. Doctors can spot incipient heart trouble, diabetes, anaemia, unwanted side-effects of medicines, before they become a major threat to health.

The trouble is that many family doctors – general practitioners as it would be more accurate to describe them now that group practices are common and the personal touch is disappearing from medicine – are operating a national illness service, not a national health service. They think in terms of what is wrong with the patient, and treat illness rather than maintain health. The older patient, aware of this, can help himself and the doctor too by taking the initiative – going for a check-up and positively seeking advice on such matters as food habits, exercise, and even mental health. A doctor gets an extra payment from the NHS for every patient on his list who is of pensionable age: no one who is retired need feel they are 'imposing' on their doctor by requiring more of his time and attention.

Ailments and illnesses

To cover the whole range of ailments, illnesses, diseases and disorders which can occur in the retirement years would take a book in itself. But there are some categories which we will touch on here: those which are familiar either because nearly everyone gets them or because (often mistakenly) everyone expects them, and those which are almost as common but are not so often mentioned, or which are taken for granted.

Eye troubles. From about middle age, everyone tends to get long-sighted, as the eye muscles weaken. Glasses are needed for reading and to see objects at close quarters. More serious eye conditions associated with old age are glaucoma and cataract. Glaucoma can cause blindness if neglected, but it should never be allowed to get that far. It arises when fluid in the eye fails to drain away, and the first symptoms are seeing haloes around lights. Later, pain from the pressure of the fluid can develop. Cataract, the chief cause of blindness in later years, is a progressive clouding of the eye lens. Early surgery gives

better results than late. Most blindness among the
retired could be prevented by early treatment.

Deafness. Nearly everyone loses acuity of hearing as the
years advance, and the decline usually starts not in older
age but in the 30s. It may simply be due to the accumulation of wax, a side product of catarrh. If not,
hearing aids can alleviate almost all deafness, and as
they are available under the NHS, it seems foolish not to
have a hearing test and to get a device if needed.
Beware of privately sold hearing aids, which are often
over-priced and no better than NHS equipment. Hearing aids have their problems, but they are better than
the withdrawal from human contact that is the alternative if deafness grows.

Cancer. Almost everyone fears cancer. But in fact, more
people die of heart disease, stroke, bronchitis and
pneumonia. Many cancers are curable; others are
preventable. The risks of lung cancer, for instance, are
very much less among non-smokers, and can be reduced
dramatically even among smokers if they drop the habit.
There is good reason for believing that bowel cancers
may be linked to chronic lack of roughage in the diet.
Breast cancer, the commonest form among women, can
usually be cured if detected early. To delay going to the
doctor out of fear, should a lump be found, is folly.

Heart. Heart disease causes 3000 deaths a week in
Britain. It is the biggest killer. Far fewer people die of
actual old age. But there is much we can do to prevent
the premature ageing of the heart which leads to heart
disease. A diet low in animal fat is important. Smoking
can be lethal and contributes heavily to heart disease
as well as lung cancer and many other illnesses. Stress of
many kinds is another cause. The best antidotes are

sensible exercise, sensible diet, sensible life-style, and no smoking.

Strokes. Raised blood pressure due to stress, over-exertion, overwork or other strains on the heart may cause a blood vessel in the brain to burst, causing a stroke, which brings whole or partial paralysis or lesser disabilities like slightly impaired speech or 'rubber legs'. Sometimes a stroke can be so minor that even the victim is hardly aware of it, but just declines a little in vigour. A series of such tiny strokes can wreak havoc, step by step, and although much research is needed into this and other causes of ageing, the best prevention is to have regular medical checks which will spot raised pressure early on, and possibly other avoidable hazards. For those who do suffer a stroke, rehabilitation to a much higher degree than was once thought possible is now known to be attainable.

Arthritis and rheumatism. These are perhaps the commonest, most painful, distressing and crippling disabilities of later years. Either wear and tear of joints in the fingers, knees, hips and spine (in declining order of frequency) is the trouble, or some disease gets into the joints, causing them to swell and ache unmercifully. Although there is a lot of study to be done on these conditions, still not fully understood, many treatments now exist to relieve the worst symptoms, including carefully graded exercises, physiotherapy, gold injections and manipulation. These diseases are painful, but they need not be crippling. Again, the best preventive is quick attention to early warning signs. Acupuncture, an unorthodox form of treatment originating in China and practised by a few specialists in Britain outside the NHS, has proved an effective treatment in some cases.

The feet. These are more vulnerable to advancing years than almost any other part of the body, yet are usually not given a thought until trouble starts. Proper footwear is essential. Soft house slippers may encourage the foot muscles to get slack, and house shoes are better. Sensible, good quality, outdoor shoes are worth the extra money. Bunions, corns and ingrowing toenails become more of a problem as one gets older. Such conditions must not be neglected, for they can lead to serious infections. Chiropody is available under the NHS. If painful feet are not treated, the whole body can be affected, because the tendency is to relieve the pain by shifting position, which can upset many other muscles. That leads, in turn, to fatigue, reduced mobility and lack of exercise, a whole vicious cycle of effect following cause which makes everything worse. All this is preventable with proper 'servicing' – something people are punctilious about giving to their cars, but which they so often fail to give to themselves.

Sleeplessness. Older people often complain of being unable to sleep well. It is not something to worry about, unless it itself arises from worry or depression over, say, a bereavement, in which case a doctor can help. But it is unpleasant. It may be a matter of not getting enough fresh air – during the day. Or it may simply arise from a changing bodily metabolism, in which case, altering one's timetable may ease the problem. Tea and coffee are both mild stimulants, so those who suffer from sleeplessness should not drink them in quantity. If pain from rheumatism or arthritis is hindering sleep, soluble aspirin can temporarily relieve it.

Incontinence. This common problem is fraught with embarrassment, which is why it is rarely mentioned.

But much can be done to cure or control it. First, see your doctor at the first sign of inability to control the bladder, even if the symptoms are slight. Doctors too are prone to the outdated notion that some afflictions are simply the normal 'wear and tear' of age, and so may show lack of concern. If so, you have the right to seek a second opinion, but it is perhaps easier to be insistent and press for relief and treatment from your own doctor. The advice, from whatever quarter, may ultimately be to have a small operation, or a course of drugs may be prescribed. If incontinence results from cystitis, most doctors seem surprisingly ignorant of this complaint considering it is one of the commonest in the book, and can do nothing. But there is a lot that you can do to alleviate the problem by avoiding the wrong liquids, and being scrupulous about hygiene. Avoid constipation. Finally, there is a very much wider range of protective garments and gadgets which can help greatly. Both the NHS and the social services can help.

Accidents. Accidents, particularly falls, become an increasing hazard in later years. Most occur in the home. Those who live alone are the most vulnerable, because there is no help about the house. Bad lighting, loose carpets, slippery surfaces should be put right. Baths should have non-slip mats. Heating sources should be guarded and special care ought to be taken if there is gas in the home. Some falls come simply from a kind of black-out, or a sudden failure of the legs, without fainting. Such occurrences seem to be caused by a momentary cut-off of blood to the brain if the head is turned suddenly or awkwardly, perhaps constricting an artery, but they are not serious and not a cause for alarm.

These are some of the physical problems which can crop up in the retirement years. Naturally, as we get older, we tend to look older and react more slowly. The body generally runs down, its functions become less efficient, more limited. There is no faddish treatment, hormone injection, monkey gland or face lift which can halt these ineluctable processes, but, as we have seen, they can be slowed, and they can be tolerable. Much of the groundwork for reasonable health in retirement can be laid in the pre-retirement years, and simple 'maintenance' thereafter. But while it is important to remain vigilant about health, it is foolish to be obsessive or over-anxious about it. There are better things to be in life, certainly in retirement, even in old age, than a hypochondriac. To an extent which the ancients realized perhaps more than modern doctors do, attitude makes an enormous difference to physical health.

Mental health

Mental health, indeed, is no less vital than the health of the body. And there are many fears which haunt those getting on in years which, understandably, cause mental distress: fear of decline, of death, of losing loved ones, of illness and pain, fear of the loneliness which desolates the lives of many older people. But like so many fears, they exist as much in the mind as in reality.

Although modern folklore has it that in older age the mind begins to crumble, this is not so at all. Intelligence does not deteriorate. If memory dwindles, it is usually helped on its way by sleeping pills and other drugs more than by age itself. Unless stricken by actual disease, or chronically abused as with alcohol, the brain does not decay. 'Senility' afflicts comparatively few: most of the conditions lumped in with it are avoidable or remediable, or would be if society devoted as much to geriatric research and treatment as it spends on nuclear submarines, gambling and cossetting the bureaucracy.

Good physical health and good mental health interact and help each other. A sensible diet ensures correct nutriment for the brain and the nervous system. An adequate family and social life and properly fulfilling leisure and occupation assist mental fitness. Interests which stimulate the mind keep it from breakdown just as effectively as physical exercise strengthens the body.

Nevertheless, distressing events obviously can trigger off acute depression. Perhaps the most common and important of these in later years is bereavement, particularly of a spouse or, if we live to a good age, possibly even of a child.

Bereavement

How to cope with bereavement? It is something to which there are many answers, and none. We all know that one day we will grieve over the loss of someone close to us, yet that loss still comes as a sorrow and a shock, and we are ill-prepared. It is because it is the last great taboo of our times, the ultimate 'unmentionable', that death, except in fiction or abstracted into celluloid and newsprint, is so shocking to us. Earlier generations saw much more of it, and so felt able to confront it in a straightforward way that we find difficult. But if the attitude adopted is right, the pain can be more bearable. Without being morbid, affairs can be arranged so that on death they are not left in total disarray, compounding the distress of natural grief

Grief is a natural reaction which should not be

suppressed. As death is not the end of retirement but of
life itself, it is not a morbid prospect, however unwelcome,
and that insight can temper the grief. Bereavement, too,
will be easier to bear unburdened by remorse. To that
end, it is important to communicate with the person who
is dying, so that one is not afterwards tormented with
thoughts of how one failed to ease their dying hours.
They are more likely to be troubled by awareness of the
grief of others than by imminence of death. Therefore,
it is not a question of struggling to find words to tell
someone that they are dying – more likely, it is they who
are seeking the opportunity to say them. It is denying
them that opportunity that is an unkindness.

Everyone must face bereavement in their own way and
find such consolations as they can. It is vital to recognize
that they do exist. As in so many things, Dr Johnson put
it perfectly. 'With regard to the sharpest and most melting
sorrow,' he wrote, 'that which arises from the loss of those
whom we have loved with tenderness, it may be observed
that friendship between mortals can be contracted on no
other terms, than that one must sometime mourn for the
other's death; and this grief will always yield to the
survivor one consolation proportionate to his affection,
for the pain, whatever it be, that he himself feels, his
friend has escaped.'

Those are extraordinarily comforting words. And it
is true that while retirement poses many problems,
there is, too, much comfort to be drawn from it. Particularly in matters of health, the encroaching years can
bring new difficulties to the conduct of life, but the
outlook need not be gloomy, all is not negative, the
path is not precipitously downhill. Much can be done
to avoid, reduce and eliminate such difficulties.

7

GETTING READY

Preparation essential

This book has had one basic, and often repeated, theme: preparation. Only preparation can ensure that retirement is fulfilled, enjoyable and reasonably free of anxiety. That applies to every sphere on which we have touched. *Personal adjustment* both of the individual and the family to retirement may fail if little or no thought is given to it: indeed, many of the growing number of pre-retirement courses now being offered suggest that active preparations should begin as early as 50. Considering *where to live* in retirement, and doing something about it if a move is planned, obviously requires forethought. *Leisure* in retirement is liable to be empty if no part-time interests or lasting friendships exist in the decades that precede it. Proper *financial provision* in retirement implies many years of pre-planning – over such matters, for example, as endowment assurance and annuities. *Finding work* in retirement is hardly something that can be done overnight. *Keeping fit* in later years is the interest paid on the accumulated capital of sensible habits and prudent care over a lifetime. For example, most diabetes in the elderly could be avoided by simple dietetic measures taken in middle life, as could many of the more distressing conditions of eyes, feet, waterworks, joints and mind. Yet, they are incorrectly assumed to be inevitable concomitants of retirement.

All this means that preparation is of the essence. It means, too, that it is ultimately for each person to make his or her own arrangements for retiring. The many forms of help that the welfare state provides – the health service, the personal social services, the educational and cultural services, the local authority services, and the voluntary services (many of which are State-funded) – are, it is true, widely available even in economically stringent times. In addition, there are important obligations towards those approaching retirement borne by employers, trade unions and professional associations – though these, regrettably, have been more shirked than shouldered so far. Yet, none of these can be more than half-effective unless the individual acknowledges the fact of his approaching retirement and consciously recognizes how vital it is that he plan ahead. Foolishly, many choose to bury their heads in the sand.

A retirement lobby

As we have seen, the transition to retirement is something that our society has not yet learned to manage well. The change at 60 or 65 is far too often a shock as unsettling as adolescence, and it need not be. Society must reform its attitudes towards its older members. In other words, it is for ordinary people to change their own attitudes. And among the people is the ever increasing 'vested interest' of the retired themselves, and the about-to-be-retired. We all tend, wrongly, to regard the elderly as not capable, not adaptable, not amenable to physical or mental challenge. So the old are patronized with often time-wasting and futile pastimes which have given old folks' clubs a somewhat pathetic image. Yet, what the old need is to be stretched, to fulfil their potential no less than the young. They are, too, just as able as the young in many ways, and often more able in that they are more motivated to make the most of opportunities. So, collectively, the 'pre-retirement lobby' could exert itself and become a powerful pressure group for bringing about the changes of attitude that must be made if the oldest fifth of our population is to cease to consist of people who are often regarded as second-class citizens. Alex Comfort says that it is not biology that creates the disabilities and penalties of old age so much as attitudes and institutions. No one can halt the biological ageing process, but we can actually reverse unnecessary 'social' ageing. And, of course, it is not State welfare that can do this. The benefits apparatus is undeniably well-intentioned, but its basic aim is to appease, to discourage people from rocking the boat. But what we really need is change. Indeed, we must cease to think in terms of age at all, but simply of needs. The 'disabilities of old age' will then be seen, quite simply, as 'disabilities': the arthritis sufferer needs help and treatment whatever his or her age. If that kind of attitude took hold, then it would no longer be a case of having to retire at some given, arbitrary, age: perfectly capable employees would no longer be put on the scrapheap simply because they had reached 60, or 62, or 65, or even 67 or 70. Nor would they, at any age, be treated differently on account of age alone, any more than people in their 20s or 40s. Such a radical transformation of social attitude could make the preparation for retirement a much less difficult and studied procedure than it is today, and would enable retirement itself to become more an integral part, a natural part, of life as a whole.

Militancy?

Those approaching retirement could prepare for it in no better way, perhaps, than by banding together to encourage new approaches of this kind. For few people are better equipped to make a concerted fuss than the older age groups. They have the time, the authority, the experience, the respectability. Militancy may sound disreputable, but if the old *were* militant, they would command respect and carry immense weight. Although this chapter concerns the responsibilities of employers and others towards retirement, no one carries more responsibility than the person who is retiring, and it is for him to make the really decisive moves. In many areas, the vehicle is already at hand, in local pre-retirement associations and branches of bodies like Age Concern and the British Association of Retired Persons.

This is not an unrealistic dream-plan for semi-permanent rejuvenation! Retired people will get older; the failings of the flesh will multiply. Nevertheless, the retired should be encouraged to fulfil themselves, and enabled to continue leading the kind of life that suits each individual, rather than compelling them to live up to some form of stereotyped life-style that is society's false expectation of them, or the false prospectus presented by society to them.

Stale policies

There are nearly 10 million British people over the age of 60. It is absurd to allot resources on the assumption that they are mostly unemployable, apathetic and witless. Yet that is the way the matter is approached – though the job is not done well even by its own lights. So, the authorities are increasingly concerned by the horrendous size of the problems that confront them – and largely misunderstand them. They see demographic realities as hurdles to surmount rather than potential to exploit. In this way, the growing numbers of retired are seen by the conventional 'wisdom' as merely equivalent to a need for more geriatric beds, or whatever. Fresher thinking might reveal that improved pensions, better facilities, and more opportunities, were easier and cheaper, quite apart from being preferable in human terms. The French, for example, have found that it costs less to send old people to good holiday hotels than to keep them in hospital. It would be nice if our own Health Department developed imaginative thinking on similar, or even more radical, lines.

Overseas examples

Indeed, there is a good deal that can be learnt from other countries. France, again, has long regarded retirement as one of the four ages of man – learning, working, retirement, dependence. There are universities which admit retired people whatever their educational qualifications and employers have to contribute two per cent of their wages bill towards the system of life-long education, which includes training for retirement. In Switzerland, there is no earnings rule, and the pensions scheme subsidizes facilities for the retired, while the trade unions are pressing for a flexible retirement age (in Britain, by awful contrast, they are merely wondering how they can get earlier retirement). In Norway, the pre-retirement association has State financial backing and encouragement. In Canada, pressure is building up not only for flexible retirement, but the abolition of compulsory retirement altogether.

In Britain, there has been much discussion in recent years of earlier retirement. This seems to be misconceived for most professional people and even for many in industry and commerce unless their work is especially taxing physically, or exceptionally unpleasant. Some of the drawbacks to early retirement have been considered already in this book, but the overriding objection to it is that society and the economy needlessly saddle themselves with a growing accumulation of able but ineligible citizens, who are largely debarred from productivity and therefore from affluence, and therefore are an economic burden on themselves and everyone else. Earlier retirement – that is, in practical terms at present, premature dependence – in an era when 65 is still barely beyond middle age, is a nonsense, and the demand for it, from certain trade unions and others, mere anachronistic mouthing of outworn slogans. The need of our times is for flexible retirement, its timing dictated by the individual and his work, plus provisions for transition into retirement by phased reductions in the time spent at work, better education for retirement, far more occupational re-training for retirement, and a complete re-thinking of retirement policies. At present, these barely exist at all. Hardly anything has been done to develop manpower policies for the older worker: the temporary employment subsidy and the job creation programme are geared towards the young. Only a handful of trainees taking Government-backed vocational training are over 40. The job-release scheme introduced in 1976, whereby people within a year of retirement can leave work on a tax free allowance provided they are replaced by an unemployed younger person, is not likely to attract any but the lower paid and unemployed. There are practically no specialist advisory and placings officers in the public employment service, as in the United States.

Company responsibilities

More and more companies are now coming to accept their responsibilities in this sphere, but they are still few. Companies should be giving their staffs the opportunity to plan for retirement in advance. They should be able to offer guidance and advice to employees who need it. Large companies, clearly, have the money and man-power to do a great deal. But even smaller companies can arrange seminars, advised, perhaps, by such bodies as the Pre-Retirement Association, which now offers 'Strategy for Retirement', a series of eight films and booklets covering all aspects of retirement and which have been commended to companies and adult edu-cation authorities by the Confederation of British Industry, the Trades Union Congress, the major political parties, and other bodies. A similar package has been devised by the British Life Assurance Trust, a com-bination of medical and life assurance expertise. Con-cerns which do adopt a positive attitude towards employees' retirement, allowing them time to attend training courses, helping them with the complexities of investment, and assisting with all the information and advice that many need, have found that the benefits outweigh the costs – which are in any case relatively small. Concerns which have yet to become aware that retirement is rather more than paying a pension can be made aware by trade unions and professional bodies either nationally or, probably more effectively, at branch level.

The kind of option that could become more common and acceptable is the provision of pre-retirement counselling, education or training linked with arrangements to enable employees to reduce their working hours gradually, over a period – the last five years of service, for example. One firm reduces the five-day week to four at 60 (for men), lopping off another day each year until full retirement is due. There are many possible variations on such a scheme. Their common object is to minimize the trauma of retirement and turn it into an opportunity. It is still too often a change that is either dreaded before it arrives or regretted afterwards. This is tragic and unnecessary.

New ideas

New groups of older 'militants', then, could be invaluable in goading or spurring the community into tackling retirement problems more constructively and imaginatively. Three examples only of the kind of thing they could consider will show what could be done. They might investigate the possibilities of setting up 'house sitting services'. Many retired people would be glad to do the useful but undemanding voluntary work of helping families which, with the wife as well as the husband in full-time employment, find it hard to keep appointments with plumbers, repairmen and other essential callers. Retired people 'sitting in' to admit workmen in such circumstances would give a useful service which could earn them extra money. A second possibility might be a campaign to provide telephones for retired people. Local authorities have ruled this out on the grounds of cost – one of those shortsighted, often false economies which have been the bane of Britain's post-war social history. The telephone can be a more valuable aid than any bus pass, cheap cinema ticket or other handout. The phone is an unrivalled antidote to loneliness, quite apart from its use in emergencies. The supposedly insuperable cost objections to universal provision for the retired are due to a lack of 'lateral thinking' by politicians and bureaucrats, or a preference for administrative convenience rather than a genuine interest in feasibility. Finally, perhaps, an American example might prove worth following: in San Diego, California, there is a Senior Exchange Service, or 'help bank', on which retired people can draw for services they need and cannot afford to buy, in return for services they can give, such as knitting, typing, free lifts and so on.

The magnitude of the need to prepare for retirement is now becoming recognized at the highest levels, and a House of Lords debate in February, 1976 was an encouraging augury for the development of more concerted, flexible, aware and imaginative policies. Speakers made many thoughtful points to underline the main theme that stopgap palliatives suitable for a society that expected the elderly to live only three or five years beyond retirement simply would no longer do. 'The retired, like the rest of us, have both a contribution to make to society and, like us all, will need to be cared for at the end,' said Baroness Young. And Lord Soper told the peers that many people wasted their later years because they felt that retirement was 'a penalty for living so long rather than an achievement of the fullness of life in the fullness of time.' The problems of retirement will increase until people have put something in the place of concentration upon the idea of death. That is the essence of the challenge that faces us.

REFERENCE SECTION

When writing to voluntary bodies for advice or information, it is suggested that a stamped, addressed envelope be sent.

Telephone numbers are given in brackets whenever possible, with trunk dialling codes.

Associations covering the whole field of retirement
Pre-Retirement Association, 19 Undine Street, London SW17 8PP (01-767 3225). Helps people prepare for retirement with books, leaflets, courses of many kinds, talks, an industrial advisory service, a wide range of information and the monthly magazine, *Pre-Retirement Choice*, obtainable direct or from newsagents.

British Association of Retired Persons, 14 Frederick Street, Edinburgh EH2 2HB (031-225 7334). A pressure group concerned with the effects of inflation on nearly-fixed incomes, and with other matters, which deserves wider support and gives members a range of informative guidance, including a useful quarterly bulletin. Takes phone calls on Monday, Wednesday and Friday mornings only.

Age Concern, Bernard Sunley House, 60 Pitcairn Road, Mitcham, Surrey (01-640 5431); Age Concern Wales, The Crescent, Caerphilly, Mid-Glamorgan CF8 1XL (0222-869224); Age Concern Scotland, 33 Castle Street, Edinburgh (031-225 5000). Age Concern is another mine of information. Issues many publications on almost all aspects of retirement and older age.

Help the Aged, 8–10 Denman Street, London W1A
2AP (01-437 2554). The largest British charity for the
old but also an articulate pressure group.

Institute of Directors Retirement Service, Drayton
House, Gordon Street, London WC1 (01-235 3601).
Available Tuesdays, Wednesdays, and Fridays only.

Consumers Association, 14 Buckingham Street, London
WC2N 6DS (01-839 1222). Subscriptions to *Which?*
and various books on wills, house-buying, job-hunting,
house extensions, where to live in retirement, and what
to do when someone dies, obtainable from 1 Caxton
Hill, Hertford SG13 7LZ (Hertford 57773).

Citizens' Advice Bureaux in most localities are invaluable starting points for anyone who is not sure how
to tackle problems or how to obtain certain information.
Public libraries and local newspapers are also most
helpful.

Another valuable service is given by the *Daily Telegraph*
Information Bureau, 135 Fleet Street, London EC4P
4BL (01-353 4242).

The Old People's Information Service, 10 Fleet Street,
London EC4 (01-353 1892). Advisory section of the
Elderly Invalids Fund, answers questions on almost every
aspect of old age.

Pre-Retirement Choice, the retirement planning magazine,
comes out monthly and is full of useful articles, short
reports and letters for the retired and those approaching
retirement.

Benevolent Institutions

Ask your public reference library for the *Charities Digest*,
which has special sections on charities for the elderly
and the disabled.

Help the Aged, 8–10 Denman Street, London W1A 2AP (01-437 2554). Britain's largest charity for older people.

Royal British Legion, 49 Pall Mall, London SW1 (01-930 8131). Helps ex-service people.

Distressed Gentlefolks Association, Vicarage Gate, London W8 (01-229 9341).

Elderly Invalids Fund, 10 Fleet Street, London EC4 (01-353 1892). Helps disabled people who do not need special hospital facilities, or needing temporary care.

Professional Classes Aid Council, 10 St. Christopher's Place, London W1M 6HY (01-935 0641).

Royal United Kingdom Beneficent Association, 6 Avonmore Road, London W14 (01-602 6274).

Friends of the Elderly and Gentlefolks Help, 42 Ebury Street, London SW1 (01-730 8263).

National Council for the Single Woman and her Dependants, 29 Chilworth Mews, London W2 3RG (01-262 1451).

National Benevolent Fund for the Aged, 12 Liverpool Street, London EC2 (01-283 3287). Instals television sets and pays licences for housebound people living alone: the applicants must be sponsored by a social worker.

Task Force, Clifford House, Edith Villas, London W14 (01-602 2627). Has volunteers who give friendship and practical help around the home with tasks like gardening, cleaning and decorating. Also produces *Save Fuel Keep Warm* which gives suggestions for fuel economy that are within reach of the average person.

Chapter 2: A Home for Life
Department of the Environment, headquarters at 2

Marsham Street, London SW1 (01-212 3434). Issues leaflets on house improvements, housing associations, renovation grants, renting, and matters to do with landlords.

Local authority housing and planning departments can give guidance about alterations, grants etc. Information available at council offices, Citizens' Advice Bureaux, housing advice centres.

Central Council for the Disabled, 34 Eccleston Square, London SW1V 1PE (01-821 1871). Publishes a booklet called *Housing Grants and Allowances for Disabled People*.

Rates: ask local authority treasurers' departments or enquiry centres for the leaflet entitled *How to Pay Less Rates*, which details eligibility to rate rebates. A similar leaflet is entitled *There's Money Off Rent*, which concerns rent allowance.

House purchase: *The Legal Side of Buying a House* (£2.15), published by the Consumer Association, 1 Caxton Hill, Hertford SG13 7LZ.

For names of local solicitors, try 'Yellow Pages' in the 'phone book or ask the Law Society, 113 Chancery Lane, London WC2A 1PL (01-242 1222). Or, best of all, get a personal recommendation.

Cut-price conveyancing organizations include the National Houseowners' Society, 19 Sheepcote Road, Harrow, Middlesex (01-427 6218); and the Property Transfer Association, 44 London Road, Kingston on Thames, Surrey (01-549 3180).

If building or converting: the Royal Institute of British Architects, 66 Portland Place, London W1 (01-580 5533). Can supply the names of local architects and have a clients' advisory service.

If letting: consult not only estate agents but large firms

and institutions like hospitals and colleges which may
have letting officers. *Parkers Property Price Guide*, 58
Parker Street, London WC1 (01-242 1961); (monthly),
available from newsagents.

A useful booklet entitled *Safety in Retirement* is available
from the Royal Society for the Prevention of Accidents,
Service and Sales Department, Cannon House, The
Priory Queensway, Birmingham B4 6BS (021-233 2461).
Gas showrooms should be able to provide a booklet
called *The Safe Use of Gas* which has information on aids
for the disabled, including a braille thermometer and
adapting controls. The local Gas Consumer Council can
help with special problems.

Electricity Consultative Councils help with special
electrical problems. Also helpful is the Electrical
Association for Women, 25 Fouberts Place, London
W1V 2AL (01-437 5212). Gives bespoke advice on any
electrical topic.

The Solid Fuel Advisory Service has local branches.
Head office is at Hobart House, Grosvenor Place,
London SW1 (01-235 2020).

Some kitchen and gardening books of use to the retired:
Cooking in a Bedsitter, by Katherine Whitehorn (Penguin).
Easy Cooking for One or Two, by Dr. Louise Davies
(Penguin). *Bedsitter Cookery* by Marguerite Patten
(Hamlyn). *Kitchen Sense for Disabled or Elderly People*, pub-
lished by Disabled Living Foundation, 346 Kensington
High Street, London W14 (01-602 2491), (£1.75, money
with order). *Eating Well in Retirement*, a book issued by the
Dairy Produce Advisory Service, Milk Marketing Board,
Thames Ditton, Surrey (01-398 4101). *The Easy Path to
Gardening*, published by the Readers Digest Association in
conjunction with the Disabled Living Foundation (£1.25

with order). This is for disabled people who wish to continue with some gardening.

Help in the home for those who have difficulty getting about is given under the WRVS Good Companions Scheme, WRVS, 17 Old Park Lane, London W1Y 4AJ (01-499 6040). For further help for the disabled, *see also* Keeping Age at Bay (below).

A. Wright and Sons Ltd., Cutlers, 16 Sidney Street, Sheffield S1 4RH (0742-22677). This firm makes garden implements for those who have difficulty in bending.

The Over Fifty Club, The Elms, 26 Broad Street, Wokingham, Berkshire RG11 1AB (0734-791179). Acquaints members with goods and services available at a discount.

Alarm-communication system for those living alone: Davis Sound Controls Ltd., Brunswick Industrial Estate, Brunswick Village, Newcastle on Tyne NE13 7BA (089426-5411).

Mobile homes (caravans): Mobile Home Residents Association, 51 Barton Street, Gloucester. There is also a free Department of the Environment leaflet entitled *Mobile Homes*.

Mutual Households Association, 41 Kingsway, London WC2 (01-836 1624). Apartments for the better-off in houses of historic or architectural interest. Accommodation is offered in return for a redeemable loan plus weekly charges.

Housing problems following bereavement: Cruse, 126 Sheen Road, Richmond Road, Surrey TW9 1UR (01-940 4818). Has a counselling and advisory service for widows and children and publishes *Caring for the Widow and her Family* (40p plus postage).

Those proposing to live abroad should consult the

Department of Health and Social Security Overseas Group, Newcastle on Tyne NE98 1YX (0632-857111). This will give general information and a specific statement of an individual's position. The DHSS also publishes leaflets on reciprocal medical and social security agreements reached with various countries. Also consult Overseas Territories Income Tax Office, Magdalen House, Trinity Road, Bootle, Merseyside L69 9BB (051-922 8711). Or local tax offices.

A Guide to U.K. Exchange Control is obtainable from the Bank of England, Threadneedle Street, London EC2 (01-601 4444). This will help those going to live abroad.

Housing associations etc.: the names of housing associations in your area are obtainable from most local housing departments. The Housing Corporation, 149 Tottenham Court Road, London W1P 0BN (01-387 9466) can give information on housing associations in different localities. The National Federation of Housing Societies, 86 Strand, London WC2R 0EG (01-836 2741) gives a nationwide guide.

The Abbeyfield Society, 35a High Street, Potters Bar, Hertfordshire (Potters Bar 43371). With many local branches, it consists of hundreds of local housing societies which enable elderly people to live in non-institutionalized family homes.

Anchor Housing Association, Oxenford House, 13–15 Magdalen Street, Oxford OX1 3BP (0865-22261).

National Association of Almshouses, Billingbear Lodge, Wokingham, Berkshire RG11 5RU (0344-54177). There are about 2000 almshouses which provide 22,000 dwellings.

The Royal British Legion Housing Association, 35

Jackson Court, Hazlemere, High Wycombe, Buckinghamshire HP15 7TX (049481-3771).
Help the Aged Housing Association, 8–10 Denman Street, London W1A 2AP (01-437 2554). One of the largest schemes of its kind.
Sutton Housing Trust, Sutton Court, Tring, Hertfordshire HP23 5BB (044282-4921).
Various religious bodies run homes for the elderly, among them the Salvation Army, the Methodist Church, the Church Army, the Jewish Welfare Board, and various Roman Catholic charities. Housing advice is given by the Catholic Housing Aid Society, 189a Old Brompton Road, London SW5 0AR (01-373 4961).
The Retirement Lease Housing Association, 24 Grosvenor Gardens, London SW1 (01-730 4141) provides tenancies of flats and bungalows while you lease your own house.
Agents for many private retirement homes include GRACE (Mrs. Gould's Residential Advisory Service for the Elderly), Leigh Corner, Leigh Hill Road, Cobham, Surrey KH11 2HW (01-266 2928). Also the Elderly Invalids' Fund, 10 Fleet Street, London EC4 (01-353 1892). For those with capital, the Active Elderly Association, Clare Park, Farnham, Surrey (0252-850681), a non-profit making body.

Chapter 3: Doing What You Want
Those interested in voluntary work could contact their local Council of Social Service, Rural Community Council or Citizens' Advice Bureau. The central body is the National Council of Social Service, 26 Bedford Square, London WC1 (01-636 4066). A volunteers' advisory service is available from the London Council of

Social Service, 68 Chalton Street, London NW1 (01-388 0241). New recruits to do voluntary work are sought by the Volunteer Centre, 29 Lower Kings Road, Berkhamsted, Hertfordshire HP4 2AB (04427-73311).

Local education authorities and libraries are a starting point for obtaining details of evening classes and other forms of adult education. The largest is the Inner London Education Authority, County Hall, London SE1 (01-633 5000). It publishes *Floodlight*, the official listing of hundreds of courses. The National Institute of Adult Education (England and Wales), 35 Queen Anne Street, London W1M (01-637 4241), publishes the *Year Book of Adult Education*, which gives details of every form of adult education. A students' inquiry service is run by The Open University, PO Box 48, Walton, Bletchley, Buckinghamshire MK7 6AB (0908-77354). The Workers' Educational Association is at 9 Upper Berkeley Street, London W1H 8BY (01-402 5608), with its London branch at 32 Tavistock Square, London WC1 (01-387 8966).

Courses on retirement and many other subjects are listed in the *Calendar of Residential Short Courses*, published by the National Institute of Adult Education twice a year. One of the newest and most pleasant holiday education centres is Earnley Concourse, Earnley Place, Chichester, Sussex (0243-670392).

Details of some (but not all) reputable correspondence schools are available from the Council for Accreditation of Correspondence Colleges, 27 Marylebone Road, London NW1 2JS (01-935 5391).

Specialists in holidays for elderly people are Saga Senior Citizens' Holidays Ltd., 119 Sandgate Road, Folkestone, Kent (0303-57300). Travel agents will have details of other holidays especially designed for the retired.

The Central Council for the Disabled, 34 Eccleston Square, London SW1V 1PE (01-821 1871), have a holiday guide for those with disabilities.

To swop your home for a holiday, try Home Interchange Ltd., PO Box 84, London NW8 (01-262 3822).

For hobby holidays, a guide is issued by Research Publications Services Ltd., Victoria Hall, Fingal Street, London SE10 (01-858 1717).

The Agents' Hotel Gazetteer for the Resorts of Europe (referred to in the text) is published by Continental Hotel Gazetteers, Travel Publications, 30 Grove Road, Beaconsfield, Buckinghamshire (04946-4040). It costs £10, and is used by many travel agents.

The main domestic tourist authorities are: British Tourist Authority, 64 St James Street, London SW1A 1NF (01-629 9191); English Tourist Board, 4 Grosvenor Gardens, London SW1W 0DV; Scottish Tourist Board, 23 Ravelston Terrace, Edinburgh EH4 3EU (031-332 2433); Wales Tourist Board, PO Box 15, Cardiff CF5 1XS (0222-27281); Northern Ireland Tourist Board, 48 High Street, Belfast BT1 2DS (0232-31221).

British Rail issues a Senior Citizens' Rail Card which provides cut-price travel for a relatively small yearly payment. British Rail has a pamphlet giving details, and an application form. For details of special travel and other facilities for the retired at holiday resorts in Britain, ask tourist boards, information centres, council offices or town halls. A pension book may be required for proof of eligibility. Alternatively, a card denoting entitlement is obtainable from DHSS Central Pensions Branch (FW), Newcastle on Tyne NR98 1YX.

Starting points for some leisure activities and interests:

Accordion Playing: National Accordion Association, Somerset House, Cranleigh, Surrey. Postal tuition from Klavar Music, 67 Highbury New Park, London N5 2EZ.

Acting: British Theatre Association, 9 Fitzroy Square, London W1.

Archery: Grand National Archery Society, 20 Broomfield Road, Chelmsford, Essex; Field Archery Association, Piers Court, Jenkins Lane, St Leonards, Tring, Hertfordshire.

Antique Collecting: The Antique Collectors Club, Clopton, Woodbridge, Suffolk.

Archaeology: Council of British Archaeology, 7 Marylebone Road, London NW1 5HA.

Astronomy: British Astronomical Association, Burlington House, Piccadilly, London W1V 0NL.

Accident Prevention: Royal Society for the Prevention of Accidents, Cannon House, The Priory Queensway, Birmingham 4.

Band Playing: British Federation of Brass Bands, 47 Hull Road, York YO1 3JP.

Bird Watching: The Royal Society for the Protection of Birds, The Lodge, Sandy, Bedfordshire SG19 2DL.

Budgerigar Breeding: The Budgerigar Society, 57 Stephyns Chambers, Bank Court, Hemel Hempstead.

Bee Keeping: British Beekeepers' Association, 55 Chipstead Lane, Riverhead, Sevenoaks, Kent TN13 2AJ.

Bell Ringing: Central Council of Church Bell Ringers, 19 Ravensgate Road, Charlton Kings, Cheltenham, Gloucestershire GL53 8NR.

Beer Mat Collecting: British Beer Mat Collectors' Society, 10 Firtree Close, Barnton, Northwich, Cheshire CW8 45L.

Boat Building: Royal Yachting Association, Victoria Way, Woking, Surrey.

Basket Making: Basket Makers' Association, Saxon House, Ickleton, Saffron Walden, Cambridgeshire.

Ballet Appreciation: Association of Ballet Clubs, 51 Vartry Road, London N15.

Beer Making: Home Brewing Centre, 120 Pinner Road, Harrow, Middlesex.

Bowls: English Bowling Association, 4 Landsdowne Crescent, Bournemouth BH1 1RX.

Brass Rubbing: Monumental Brass Society, 57 Leeside Crescent, London NW11.

Calligraphy: Society of Scribes and Illuminators, 6 Queen Square, London WC1.

Camping: Camping Club of Britain and Northern Ireland, 11 Lower Grosvenor Place, London SW1W 0EY.

Candle Making: Candle Makers Suppliers, 4 Beaconsfield Terrace Road, London W14.

Caravanning: Caravan Club, East Grinstead House, East Grinstead, Sussex.

Card Games: easy-to-see cards for those with weak sight from Waddington Playing Card Co. Ltd., Wakefield Road, Leeds LS10 3TP.

Car Restoration: Veteran Car Club of Great Britain, 14 Fitzhardinge Street, London W1; Vintage Sports Car Club, 121 Russell Road, Newbury, Berkshire RG14 5JX.

Cartooning: correspondence courses from Aldermaston College, Reading RG7 4PF.

Cat Breeding: Governing Council of the Cat Fancy, c/o Mrs. W. Davis, Dovefields, Petworth Road, Witley, Godalming, Surrey.

Chess: British Chess Federation, 4 The Close, Norwich

NR1 4DH; also at Juniper Cottage, South Park Crescent, Gerrards Cross, Buckinghamshire; British Correspondence Chess Association, 83 Waldegrave Road, Coventry, or, 28 Canonbury Park North, London N1.

Choral Singing: National Association of Choirs, 48 Crossfield Road, Cheadle Hulme, Cheshire SK8 5PE.

Cine Filming: Institute of Amateur Cinephotographers, 63 Woodfield Lane, Ashstead, Surrey.

Coin Collecting: British Association of Numismatic Societies, 51a Old Park Road, London N13; British Numismatic Society, Warburg Institute, Woburn Square, London WC1H 0AB.

Conjuring: The Magic Circle, 84 Chenies Mews, London WC2.

Cookery: Cordon Bleu Cookery School, 114 Marylebone Lane, London W1.

Correspondence: Conversation Through Correspondence, 6 Bollin Court, Macclesfield Road, Cheshire SK9; Sundial Society, 3 Perrycroft, Windsor, Berks.

Croquet: Croquet Association, Hurlingham Club, London SW6.

Cycling: Cyclists Touring Club, 69 Meadrow, Godalming, Surrey. British Cycling Federation, 70 Brompton Road, London SW13 1E.

Darts: National Darts Association, Secretary Mr. C. Burden, Trevanion Road, Weybridge, Cornwall.

Dog Breeding: Kennel Club, 1–4 Clarges Street, London.

Dog Training: Royal Society for the Prevention of Cruelty to Animals, The Manor House, Horsham, Sussex; Peoples' Dispensary for Sick Animals, South Street, Dorking, Surrey.

Draughts: English Draughts Association, 281 Broxtowe Lane, Aspley, Nottingham NG8 5NE.

Engraving: Royal Society of Painters, Etchers and Engravers, 26 Conduit Street, London W1.

Environmental Conservation: Conservation Society, 12 London Street, Chertsey, Surrey KT16 8AA; National Trust, 42 Queen Anne's Gate, London SW1; National Trust for Scotland, 5 Charlotte Square, Edinburgh EH2 4DU; Council for the Protection of Rural England, 4 Hobart Place, London SW1.

Embroidery: Embroiderers Guild, 2 Greycoat Place, London SW1.

Escort Services for Children: WRVS, 17 Old Park Lane, London W1; National Federation of Womens' Institutes, 39 Eccleston St., London SW1.

First Aid: St John Ambulance Brigade, 1 Grosvenor Crescent, London SW1; British Red Cross Society, 9 Grosvenor Crescent, London SW1X 7EJ.

Fish Breeding: Federation of British Aquatic Societies, 18 The Barons, St Margarets, Twickenham TW1 2AP.

Fishing: National Federation of Anglers, 87 Green Lane, Derby.

Flower Arranging: National Association of Flower Arrangement Societies, 21a Denbigh Street, London SW1V 2HF.

Folk Dancing: English Folk Dance and Song Society, 2 Regents Park Road, London NW1.

Gardening: Royal Horticultural Society, Vincent Square, London SW1 2PE; National Society of Leisure Gardeners, 22 High Street, Flitwick, Bedfordshire.

Genealogy: Heraldry Society, 28 Museum Street, London WC1A 1LH; Society of Genealogists, 37 Harrington Gardens, London SW7.

Golf: English Golf Union, 12a Denmark Street, Wokingham, Berkshire RG11 2BE.

Handbell Ringing: Central Council of Church Bell Ringers, Denmark House, Guildford, Surrey.

Historical Societies: Historical Association, 59a Kennington Park Road, London SE11 4JH.

Hospital Broadcasting: Hospital Broadcasting Association Studio Centre, 574 Winchester Road, Southampton.

International Societies: see Associations in 'Yellow Pages' especially London directories.

Jigsaw Puzzles: British Jigsaw Puzzle Library, 25 Kidbroke Grove, London SE3 0LE; advice on starting a club from Mrs. J. A. Cox, 5 Richmond Drive, Watford, Hertfordshire.

Marquetry: The Marquetry Society, 113 Kingway, Petts Wood, Kent BR5 1PP.

Matchbox Collecting: British Matchbox and Booklet Society, The Bungalow, Pine Ridge County School, Esher Road, Old Dean Estate, Camberley, Surrey.

Mineral Collecting: list of clubs in *Gems* magazine, 84 High Street, Broadstairs, Kent.

Model Making: British Model Soldier Society, 22 Priory Gardens, Hampton, Middlesex; Model Railway Club, 4 Calshot Street, London N1; Society of Model Aeronautical Engineers, 54 Belgrove Road, London E11 3QW; Miniature Armoured Fighting Vehicle Association, 15 Berwick Avenue, Heaton Mersey, Stockport, Cheshire SK4 3AA.

Music Appreciation: classes given by Workers Educational Association, 9 Upper Berkeley Street, London W1H 8BY.

Musical Instruments: The Galpin Society, Rose Cottage, Bois Lane, Chesham Bois, Buckinghamshire.

Opera Singing: National Operatic and Dramatic Association, 1 Crestfield Street, London WC1H 8AU.

Orchestral Playing: National Federation of Music Societies, 1 Montague Street, London WC1B 5BF.

Organ Playing: The Organ Club, 6 Chalcot Gardens, London NW3 4YB.

Photography: Camera Club, 8 Great Newport Street, London WC2.

Play Helping: Pre-School Playgroups Association, Alford House, Aveline Street, London SE11 5DH.

Prison Visiting: National Association of Prison Visitors, 47 Hartington Street, Bedford.

Probation Voluntary Work: Probation and After Care Department, Home Office, Romney House, Marsham Street, London SW1.

Puppetry: British Puppet and Model Theatre Guild, 18 Maple Road, Yeading, Hayes, Middlesex.

Rabbit Breeding: British Rabbit Council, Purefory House, 7 Kirkgate, Newark on Trent, Nottinghamshire.

Railway Societies: Railway Correspondence and Travel Society, 95 Chestnut Avenue, London E7 0JF; The Railway Club, 112 High Holborn, London WC1; Railway and Canal Historical Society, 174 Station Road, Wylde Green, Sutton Coldfield, Warwickshire.

Rambling: Ramblers Association, 1–4 Crawford Mews, York Street, London W1H 1PT.

Sculpture: Royal Society of British Sculptors, 108 Old Brompton Road, London SW7 3RA.

Shell Collecting: British Shell Collectors' Club, 110 Richmond Road, Gillingham, Kent; Conchological Society of Great Britain, 51 Wychwood Avenue, Luton, Bedfordshire LU2 7HP.

Stamp Collecting: British Philatelic Association, 1 Whitehall Place, London SW1; National Philatelic Association, same address.

Swimming: Amateur Swimming Association, Harold Fern House, Derby Square, Loughborough LE11 0AL.

Table Tennis: English Table Tennis Association, 21 Claremont, Hastings, Sussex; Table Tennis Association of Wales, 198 Cyncoed Road, Cardiff.

Tape Recording: Federation of British Tape Recordists and Clubs, 33 Fairlawnes, Maldon Road, Wallington, Surrey.

Toy Libraries: Toy Libraries Association, 10 Gunthorpe Street, London E1 7RW.

Toy Making: British Toymakers' Guild, 32–4 Ridgway, London SW19 4QW.

Wine Making: English Vineyards Association, The Vineyards, Cricks Green, Felsted, Essex CN6 3JT.

Waterways Restoration: Inland Waterways Protection Society, Gorse-side, Cartledge Lane, Holmfield, Sheffield S18 5SB.

Chapter 4: The Money Side

Pensions. There are many useful publications including *The Complete Guide to Pensions and Superannuation* by Dryden Gilling-Smith (Penguin); *Know Your New Pension Rights* (*Sunday Telegraph*, 70p). The Company Pensions Information Centre, 7 Old Park Lane, London W1Y 3LJ, publishes *How to Understand Your Pension Scheme*, and *How a Pension Scheme Works*, both free.

Details of pensions, supplementary benefits and other State payments are given in leaflets available at post offices and social security offices, and in the *Supplementary Benefits Handbook*, available from Her Majesty's Stationery Offices. There is also *The Penguin Guide to Supplementary Benefits*, and the *Guide to the Social Services* published by the Family Welfare Association whose central office is at 501 Kingland Road, London E8 (01-254 6251). *Money Which?* is a most useful publication, and is available from the Consumers' Association, 1 Caxton Hill, Hertford SG13 7LZ (Hertford 57773), and most reference libraries. Income tax offices have a free leaflet entitled *Income Tax and the Elderly*.

A booklet called *Making Your Will?* is issued by the Law Society, 113 Chancery Lane, London WC2A 1PZ (01-242 1222).

Details of various forms of National Savings are available at post offices. *Investing in National Savings* (Booklet SL 480) is a complete guide, published by the Department of National Savings, Blythe Road, London W14 (01-603 2000).

The Over Fifty Club, The Elms, 26 Broad Street, Wokingham, Berkshire RG11 1AB (0734-791179) offers no-medical insurance policies for those aged 50 to 72. Penguin publish a *Guide to Insurance*.

Investments: *Investing for Income* is a useful booklet available from B. G. Eales (Insurance Brokers), Calthorpe Road, Edgbaston, Birmingham. Penguin publish a *Complete Guide to Investment*.

If you need an accountant try the 'Yellow Pages' sections of the telephone directories, get a personal recommendation, or ask The Secretary, Institute of Chartered Accountants of England and Wales, Moorgate Place, London EC2 (01-628 7060); Institute of Chartered Accountants, Scotland, 66 Cannon Street, London EC4 (01-248 1427).

Associations which can give advice include the National Federation of Old Age Pensioners' Associations, 91 Preston New Road, Blackburn, Lancashire BB2 6BD (0254-52606). It has 1000 branches dealing with pension problems and also has a social side. Some localities have Financial Advice Bureaux to supplement Citizens' Advice Bureaux. The Pre-Retirement Association, 19 Undine Street, London SW17 8PP (01-767 3225) has among its members firms which can give financial advice. The Citizens' Rights Office, 1 Macklin Street, London WC2 (01-405 4517) advises on entitlements, legal problems, tenancy disputes etc. The National Federation of Claimants' Unions, 44 Havelock Street, Birmingham 20, helps people with welfare entitlements. *The Daily Telegraph*, 135 Fleet Street, London EC4 (01-353 4242) publishes *Living with Capital Transfer Tax* (45p; 55p by post; £1 inclusive for two copies).

Chapter 5: Work

Useful publications include: *Working for Yourself: a Daily Telegraph Guide* (£1.35); *Changing Your Job*, published by *The Daily Telegraph* and Kogan Page Ltd. (£1.20); *Someone Like You Can Help*, a good guide to the 600 voluntary organizations and the work they offer, published by the London Council of Social Service, 68 Chalton Street, London NW1 1JR (01-388 0241); *Mind Your Own Business*, published by Distributive Industry Training Board, Information Services Division, Maclaren House, Talbot Road, Manchester, M32 0FP (061-872 2494).

The Employment Fellowship, Drayton House, Gordon Street, London WC1H 0BE (01-387 1828) has centres where work suited to the individual can be done to supplement income and provide companionship.

British Voluntary Services Overseas, 10 Belgrave Square, London SW1 (01-235 3601) provides voluntary, unpaid executive services in developing countries. Part Time

Careers, 10 Golden Square, London W1 (01-437 3103).
The Homebound Craftsmen Trust, 25a Holland Street,
London W8 (01-937 3924) accepts high quality goods
made by people unable to get ordinary jobs. Much can
also be sold by members of Womens' Institutes through
their markets.

The Government's Training Opportunities Scheme
(TOPS), though geared to the young, does in fact have
no upper age limit. Details are available from local Job
Centres.

'Yours', PO Box 126, Watford, Hertfordshire, has a list
of work centres and employment bureaux for the
retired. Similar information is available from the Pre-
Retirement Association and Age Concern (*see* Associations). Senior Service Bureau, 2/385 Kings Road,
London SW10 (01-351 1071).

Ideas and advice from the Institute of Small Business,
Tower Suite, 1 Whitehall Place, London SW1 (01-
930 4001).

Information on retailing from the National Economic
Development Council, 21 Millbank, London SW1
(01-211 3000).

If opening a shop, you can get legal advice, preferential
insurance and other help from the National Union of
Small Shopkeepers, Westminster Buildings, Theatre
Square, Nottingham (0602-46319).

Other trade associations include the National Federation of Retail Newsagents, 2 Bridewell Place, London
EC4V 6AR (01-353 6816); Retail Confectioners' Association, 53 Christchurch Avenue, London N12 (01-
445 6344); Federation of Retail Tobacconists, 546
Commercial Road, London E1 0JE (01-790 7411).

Those going into business will need insurance on

premises, stock etc.: insurance brokers are listed in the 'Yellow Pages'. Also, information can be obtained from The Secretary, Corporation of Insurance Brokers, 15 St Helen's Place, London EC3 (01-588 4387).

Chapter 6: Keeping Age at Bay

Useful publications include: *Health in Old Age* and *Coping with Disablement*, both available from the Consumers' Association, 1 Caxton Hill, Hertford SG13 7LZ (Hertford 57773); *Home Care for the Elderly*, from the Health Education Council, 78 New Oxford Street, London W1 (01-637 1881); *How to Avoid Falls*, published by the Royal Society for the Prevention of Accidents, Cannon House, The Priory Queensway, Birmingham 4 (021-233 2461); *Basic Guide to a Green Old Age*, which in six brief pages contains a fund of good nutritional sense and some interesting food ideas, published by Henry Doubleday Research Association, Covent Lane, Bocking, Braintree, Essex (0376-24083). Other sources of nutritional advice: British Nutrition Foundation, 15 Belgrave Square, London SW1Q 8PS (01-235 4904); Geriatric Nutrition Unit, Queen Elizabeth College, Campden Hill Road, London W8 (01-937 5411).

Hearing: Royal National Institute for the Deaf, 105 Gower Street, London WC1E 5AH (01-387 8033). Gives a free hearing aid test service and will advise on the most suitable hearing aid. The Institute also produces aids for television, radio, telephone and doorbells. Offices of the Department of Health and Social Security issue a leaflet entitled *General Guidance to Hearing Aid Users*. Hearing aids can be obtained from hospitals or bought privately, though you should first ensure that the dealer is reputable.

Sight: much assistance can be obtained from the Health and Social Services. Guidance, help, advice and training are available at the Royal National Institute for the Blind, 224 Great Portland Street, London W1 (01-388 1266); National Library for the Blind, 35 Great Smith Street, London SW1 (01-222 2725), also at 5 St John Street, Manchester (061-834 0432). Guide Dogs for the Blind, 113 Uxbridge Road, London W5 (01-567 7001).

For those both deaf and blind: National Deaf and Blind Helpers' League, Market Chambers, Cathedral Square, Peterborough PE1 1XU (0733-73511).

For the handicapped: British Red Cross Society, 9 Grosvenor Crescent, London SW1X 7EJ (01-235 5454), and local branches everywhere; Central Council for the Disabled, 34 Eccleston Square, London SW1V 1PE (01-821 1871); St John Ambulance, 1 Grosvenor Crescent, London SW1 (01-235 5231) with many local branches, provides publications and courses on nursing and first aid. Disabled Living Foundation, 346 Kensington High Street, London W14 8NS (01-602 2491) can give help on all kinds of suitable aids for various conditions.

Scottish Information Service for the Disabled, 18 Claremont Crescent, Edinburgh EH7 4QD (031-556 3882). The Chest, Heart and Stroke Association, Tavistock House, Tavistock Square, London WC1H 9JE (01-387 3012) has an information and welfare service. SSAFA, 27 Queen Anne's Gate, London SW1 (01-839 4131) is interested in the welfare of retired service personnel.

Wireless for the Bedridden Society, 20 Wimpole Street, London W1 (01-935 0949). In many localities, voluntary organizations repair radios used by disabled people.

Special accommodation for handicapped people: the best known body is Cheshire Foundation Homes, 7 Market Mews, London W1 (01-499 2665) which has homes all over the world.

John Grooms Housing Association, 10 Gloucester Drive, London N4 (01-802 7272) has purpose-built flats for those confined to wheelchairs.

Work for the handicapped: Remploy, 415 Edgware Road, London NW2 (01-452 8020).

Help for those who need nursing but have serious money problems: Elderly Invalids Fund, 10 Fleet Street, London EC4 (01-353 1892).

Nursing homes: Friends of the Elderly, 42 Ebury Street, London SW1W oLZ (01-730 8263); Distressed Gentle-folks' Aid Association, Vicarage Gate, London W8 (01-229 9341).

Reaching aids to help people who find it difficult to reach light articles, Helping Hand Co., Church Road, Sandhurst, Kent TN18 5NT.

Private health insurance: the best way to obtain cover is through a provident insurance scheme. You must join as soon as possible and certainly before retirement. The main provident organizations are: British United Provident Association, Provident House, Essex Street, London W2 (01-353 9451); Private Patients' Plan, Tunbridge Wells, Kent (0892-26255); Western Provident Association, Culver Street, Bristol (0272-23495).